OPERA GUIDE 44

Gwynne Howell in the title role with Elizabeth Connell as Judith in the ENO production by Glen Byam Shaw (photo: Reg Wilson)

This Opera Guide is sponsored by

44

The Stage Works of Béla Bartók

Opera Guide Series Editor: Nicholas John

John Calder · London
Riverrun Press · New York

Published in association with English National Opera

COPYRIGHT DATA

First published in Great Britain, 1991, by
John Calder (Publishers) Ltd,
9-15 Neal Street, London WC2H 9TU

First published in the U.S.A., 1991, by
Riverrun Press Inc., 1170 Broadway,
New York, NY 10001

English National Opera receives financial assistance from the Arts Council of Great Britain.

Typeset in Plantin by Maggie Spooner Typesetting, London NW5.

Printed in Great Britain by Billing & Sons Ltd, Worcester.

CONTENTS

LIST OF ILLUSTRATIONS

Cover Design by Anita Boyd incorporating a photograph of Bartók
Frontispiece: Gwynne Howell and Elizabeth Connell, ENO, 1978 (photo: Reg Wilson)

Picture research by Ian Stones

Images of the Self: 'Duke Bluebeard's Castle'

Paul Banks

When on May 24, 1918, *Duke Bluebeard's Castle* was performed for the first time — seven years after its composition — the majority of Hungarian critics responded positively to Bartók's music, but castigated the symbolist libretto by Béla Balázs. A notable exception was Zoltán Kodály who wrote in *Nyugat* (West), the leading Hungarian periodical supporting progressive cultural ideals, that Balázs' text was 'one of his finest, most poetic concepts', arguing that in the fusion of text and music 'the arc of drama and the parallel arc of music fortify each other in a grand double rainbow'. Perhaps today, in the wake of the post-modernist reassessment of *fin-de-siècle* art, it is possible to appreciate both the insight offered by Kodály and the extent to which the composer and librettist were seeking to articulate certain existential issues which suffuse the human condition.

The question of personal identity lurks beneath the surface of the opera: Judith's opening of forbidden doors is as much an attempt to understand the personality of her betrothed as is Elsa's asking the forbidden question in *Lohengrin*. For the librettist of *Duke Bluebeard's Castle* that question had no easy answer. Born Herbert Bauer in 1884, he adopted the pseudonym Béla Balázs when at the age of sixteen he published his first poems in a local newspaper, but although he continued to use it in all his professional work, he always signed himself 'Herbert' to his closest friends. The choice of nom-de-plume was significant, a clear indication of the desire of the young Jewish writer from a predominantly German cultural background to identify with the indigenous Hungarian culture, an attempt to overcome a feeling of isolation. He later wrote 'over my early childhood spread the shadow of a certain melancholy — *loneliness*' and shortly before his death he reflected that 'the most painful human suffering is loneliness'. Such an awareness must have been intensified by his ethnic and cultural environment (not unlike that of Gustav Mahler a generation earlier in Moravia) but this feeling of alienation also found increasingly powerful expression in the writings of other Hungarian poets such as Endre Ady (1877-1919), and even before he collaborated with Balázs, Bartók had written to his mother:

> I am a lonely man! . . . I may have friends in Budapest . . . yet there are times when I suddenly become aware of the fact that I am absolutely alone! And I prophesy, I have a foreknowledge, that this spiritual loneliness is to be my destiny. I look about me in search of the ideal companion, and yet I am fully aware that it is a vain quest. Even if I should ever succeed in finding someone, I am sure that I would soon be disappointed. [10 September, 1905]

Six years later Balázs' libretto would offer Bartók the opportunity to embody such feelings in a uniquely powerful artistic portrayal of human isolation.

It was through Kodály that the two men met. In 1902 Balázs was awarded a scholarship to study at the prestigious Eötvös Collegium in Budapest, a training institute for particularly gifted teachers, and his room-mate there was Kodály. The two students formed an enduring friendship and participated together in a number of cultural projects including the Thalia Society, founded in 1904 at the suggestion of György Lukács (the future marxist philosopher and literary critic) in order to promote the propagation of modern drama in Hungary. In 1906-7 they travelled to Berlin and then Paris where Kodály discovered the music of Debussy: through him Bartók gained access to one of the crucial musical influences on his early style. However, it had been Kodály's interest in Hungarian folksong which had been instrumental in establishing his friendship with Bartók in 1905, and both he and Bartók subsequently used the Bauer home at Szeged as a base for folksong collecting expeditions. Balázs accompanied Bartók on one such trip in 1906, and wrote of the young composer in his diary:

> He is naive and gawky. A twenty-five-year-old *Wunderkind*. There is an admirable, quiet tenacity in him. He is a weak, scrawny, sickly wisp of a man, but, even when I was very tired, he still urged me, drove me on — onward to collect more. He plays beautifully, composes fine things . . . He is the captive of his talent.

Hungarian folk-ballad style eventually formed the model for the text of *Duke Bluebeard's Castle*, and in the years up to 1911 Bartók gradually forged a personal idiom, fusing the apparently disparate influences of Hungarian folk music, and modern Western art music, particularly that of Debussy, into a new musical language of enormous potential. When Ferruccio Busoni, one of the advocates of musical modernism, heard the innovatory Bagatelles, Op. 6 in 1908 he commented: 'Endlich etwas wirklich neues' (At last something truly new).

Balázs was simultaneously trying to develop a new dramatic idiom which would 'show the inner images, the struggles that are inner dialogues' and manifest 'the effects that are the silent visionlike images within the self'. From the outset he rejected the notion of realism and argued in favour of a drama which embodied the transcendental forces at work on man: when the text of the opera was first published in book form in 1912 it was as one of three *Mystery Plays*. Its origins lay in an aborted one-act stage work entitled *Don Juan and Bluebeard* which was probably begun in 1908. How much of this was retained in the revised version is unclear, but in any case the final text picked up and explored themes which had already appeared in Balázs' published writing. The bleak, fatalistic vision of a world in which significant relationships between men and women are impossible had already been adumbrated in his first fairy-tale to appear in print, *The Silence*. Although responsive to the physical and intellectual attractions of women, Balázs' attitudes towards them contained contradictions: he advocated universal women's suffrage and explored the problem of the role of the educated woman in bourgeois society in his play *Doctor Margit Szélpál* (1906). But no satisfactory answer is offered to that problem — family or career — and in 'Dedication to a Friend', the first poem of the collection *The Wanderer Sings* (1911), Balázs argues that friendship between men is superior to love between man and woman. In his review of the collection Lukács endorsed this view, adding that 'man for woman and woman for man is forever unobtainable', thus echoing the theme of *Duke Bluebeard's Castle*.

Bartók's attitudes towards women, at this stage in his life, seem to have been at least as contradictory. In a letter to his mother he had commented:

> Women should be accorded the same liberties as men. Women ought to be free to do the same things as men, or men ought not to be free to do things women aren't supposed to do — I used to believe this to be so for the sake of equality. However, after giving the subject much thought I

Béla Bartók (seated right) with the original cast in costume as Judith (Olga Haselbeck) and Bluebeard (Oszkar Kalman) and the director Dezső Zádor after the première at the Royal Hungarian Opera House, May 24, 1918. (photo: Collection Ferenc Bónis, Budapest)

have come to believe that men and women are so different in mind and body that it may not be such a bad idea after all to demand from women a greater degree of chastity. But though these considerations might lead one to favour more restraints for women, one has to take into account what happens all too often as a result . . . . And so I come back to where I started: equal standards for men and women.

Yet in all three of his stage works women are portrayed in a relatively unfavourable light, as posing the forbidden question, as failing (initially) to respond to an offer of genuine human contact (in *The Wooden Prince*, a pantomime to a scenario by Balázs), and as whore — though it has to be said that in the last, the ballet *The Miraculous Mandarin*, that bleak portrayal of the human condition, men are seen in no more flattering a light.

But the libretto of *Duke Bluebeard's Castle* did more than merely explore attitudes and beliefs with which Bartók had an innate sympathy. In its handling of myth and language, the fusion of the archaic (folktale and folk-ballad metres) with modern elements (psychological analysis and the post-Maeterlinckian techniques of symbolist drama) it paralleled the integration of primeval folk music (particularly pentatonic elements) with contemporary art music (diatonic and chromatic) which by 1911 Bartók had miraculously achieved. In other ways it was ideally suited to a composer's first attempt at opera. As the two *dramatis personae* are explicitly portrayed less as individuals

9

The Hungarian State Opera's 1952 production designed by Gusztáv Oláh. (photo: Archiv Universal Edition)

than as archetypes, Bartók did not have to forge *ab origine* a fully-fledged technique of operatic characterisation, but instead focused on differentiating Bluebeard and Judith. Overall Bluebeard's vocal line shows strong pentatonic characteristics which it shares with the music associated with the castle; the relative smoothness of the resulting melodic contours helps to stress that Bluebeard never manifests his evident capacity for cruelty and violence. It is through Judith that more chromatic and angular melodic lines are introduced into Bluebeard's domain, although at times (for instance, at the central climax of the opera), she adopts Bluebeard's melodic idiom. Here, at the opening of the fifth door, Bluebeard proudly reveals his lands to her accompanied by resounding triads for the full orchestra doubled by the organ. Judith acknowledges the vista, and in doing so uses an unadulterated pentatonic phrase. But Bartók suggests that she is disturbed and confused by this insight into Bluebeard's soul and that it distances her from him: instead of adopting the 'white-notes' of the unequivocal C major of the orchestra's final chord, Judith sings to a tonally remote 'black-note' pentatonic scale. The irony of her response is perfectly captured.

On a larger scale, Balázs not only carefully controls the relative importance of the two figures, Judith gradually receding as the recesses of Bluebeard's psyche are revealed, but he also provides Bartók with a well-defined dramatic structure made up of clearly differentiated episodes within a strongly goal-oriented narrative. Moreover a clear symmetry controls the seven episodes devoted to the opening of the doors. The first two and the last two doors open to reveal negative components of Bluebeard's soul: his potential for cruelty and violence, his sadness, his memories. The light from the first two doors is feeble, and the opening of the sixth and seventh doors darkens the hall. The

Zoltán Fülöp's designs for the Hungarian State Opera's 1958 production showing the influence of Wieland Wagner's post-war regime at Bayreuth. (photo: Archiv Universal Edition)

three central doors reveal more positive aspects of the human soul: in these cases it is Bluebeard who urges Judith to open them. The light which they reveal is stronger, and in the case of doors four and five, it comes from outside the castle.

Although the arch-like form which results from this arrangement was much favoured in Bartók's later works, it finds relatively little reinforcement in the music of the opera, though the opening material, used to portray the castle itself, returns at the end. Perhaps the composer felt that an overt mirroring of the symmetry of the libretto through a complex system of musical reminiscences would be tautological. Whatever the reason, the music is much more concerned with vividly characterising each episode — the martial glare of the armoury, the glittering beauty of the treasure room, the oppressive sadness of the lake of tears — and allowing the material of each episode to evolve organically. This is particularly apparent as Judith first explores the castle: a sombre pentatonic *ostinato* unwinds in the cellos and basses, later spawning countermelodies and changing its own contours, providing a fascinating musical process which matches Judith's growing and changing perception of the building.

Rather surprisingly for a post-Wagnerian, post-Straussian work of this period *Duke Bluebeard's Castle* makes relatively little use of recurring motifs. But the most obvious exception is both powerfully direct and all-pervasive. It emerges for the first time as Judith gropes her way around the walls of the hall and realises that they are damp: piercing semitones cut through the texture. It is only later that the symbolic significance of this disturbing dislocation of the otherwise pentatonic texture of the opening is revealed, when semitone discords are repeatedly associated with the blood which pollutes all of

11

Bluebeard's possessions. Yet the interval clearly represents far more — fear, guilt, pain and sadness — and it gradually dominates the texture as Judith taunts the duke into giving her the key to the last door. It continues to resonate in the bitonal textures towards the end — a sombre reminder of the failure of the two characters to establish a true bond. Finally all that is left is the primeval pentatonicism of the opening.

Duke Bluebeard's Castle represents a remarkably fortunate and apposite conjunction of text and music, so it is surprising that initially it was not intended for Bartók, and even led a shadowy existence as a spoken play. Balázs offered it as a libretto to Kodály, probably in 1910, but the composer 'could not feel an affinity with it'. However, Bartók responded much more enthusiastically and when Balázs visited Kodály and Bartók during their summer vacation in the Swiss alps in 1911, he found Bartók hard at work on the opera, and recorded his impressions:

> A most moving and wonderful man . . . . He possesses an incredible magical dignity . . . . There is a wonderful paradox in his appearance. His figure, face, movements are like a rococo prince's, and yet there is a certain titanic dignity about him. A rococo titan!

The work was completed in September of that year and entered for a competition organised by the Lipótváros Casino in Budapest. But it was rejected as unperformable, and the première delayed until 1918. After only eight performances it was withdrawn, and was not heard again in Hungary until 1936. Despite the success of the pantomime *The Wooden Prince*, its successor, *The Miraculous Mandarin*, was not performed in Hungary during the composer's life-time. This failure to establish himself on the Hungarian stage persuaded Bartók to withdraw from composition for the theatre. Nevertheless it seems that he did not entirely give up his ambitions in this field. In 1930 he wrote to Balázs — by then a political refugee forced into exile by Horthy's right-wing regime in Hungary — asking for permission that *The Wooden Prince* and *Duke Bluebeard's Castle* might be performed without any indication of their librettist's identity: only by such a ploy was there any chance that the works might be heard in Budapest. At the same time — perhaps out of politeness, since there could have been no chance of a production in Hungary — Bartók asked if Balázs had any suitable opera libretto available. He did not, but sent Bartók a scenario for a modern pantomime, probably *A Little Girl in a Big City*, an erotic, expressionist plot. In the light of Bartók's experience with *The Miraculous Mandarin*, it is hardly surprising that the project made no further progress. The most significant memorial to their collaboration remained a solitary, intense and sombre opera — one of the twentieth century's most outstanding contributions to the genre.

Bartók and 'World Music'

Simon Broughton

'Velvet forests, silken meadows, silver sounds of rivers running, far away majestic mountains.' The description of Bluebeard's kingdom might be of Bartók's birthplace, Transylvania. He was born in Nagyszentmiklós, now the Romanian town of Sînnicolau Mare about 60 kilometres from Timişoara. Here it is the Transylvania of 'silken meadows' rather than the 'majestic mountains' of the Carpathians, which loosely define its borders to the south and east.

Transylvania has had a three-star rating in the world music guide since Bartók and Kodály started collecting there in 1907. Even then they discovered older performing styles and archaic material that had disappeared elsewhere. The difference is yet more marked today, when village music in its traditional form is harder and harder to find in twentieth-century Europe.

Bartók's birthplace is in the Banat, an area distinct from Transylvania proper, with its own musical tradition that has recently become all the rage in Romania. Its fast and furious music is heard at weddings, in bars and from radios all over the country.

One of the reasons for the riches and special character of Transylvanian music is the ethnic mix. 'The racial impurity', said Bartók, 'is definitely beneficial.' In fact Transylvania has a mini-world-music culture of its own. Romanians, Hungarians, Saxons, Serbians and Gipsies have lived together for hundreds of years. Musical styles have rubbed off on each other and at the same time have stood as a statement of identity. A chameleon, says Patrick Leigh Fermor, placed on a coloured population-map of the Banat, would explode.

Bartók's paternal grandmother came from a Serbian family, and his father was headmaster of an agricultural school for German Catholic boys. A keen amateur musician, he played the cello, organized an amateur orchestra and composed some dance music. Bartók's mother (of German extraction) was a piano teacher and it was she who began his musical education.

The middle classes and the peasantry met, culturally, only at the most superficial level and so Bartók was unaware of the musical riches that surrounded him. He wrote later that he received no folkloristic impressions in Nagyszentmiklós or the other rural towns in which he spent his childhood. His first musical experiences were of his mother's dance pieces, the ubiquitous gipsy music and the performances of his father's amateur orchestra. At a local restaurant he heard Hungarian popular songs mixed with opera extracts by Verdi, Rossini, Donizetti and Meyerbeer. While the other guests went on eating and drinking the young Bartók listened with complete absorption.

Bartók's musical talents showed themselves early. At the age of four he could pick out around forty tunes on the piano. He had perfect pitch and an instinctive sense of rhythm. In 1888, when he was seven, his father died and his mother found a job as a teacher in Nagyszőllős (now Vinogradov, just over the Hungarian border in the Soviet Ukraine). Once again Bartók was living unaware in a territory that he was subsequently to find very rich in music.

Here he started to compose (mainly dance tunes for the piano) and in 1894, with his characteristic passion for collecting and classifying, he compiled a

13

catalogue of his compositions. Each is listed with its title, its dedication, Bartók's age when it was written and the place of composition. Most important is the twenty-minute piano piece *A Duna folyása* (*The Course of the Danube*), whose title is underlined three times in the notebook. It is obvious that the young composer attached great importance to it as its original opus 20 is crossed out and corrected into opus 1. He played it with the first movement of the 'Waldstein' Sonata at his first public appearance, a charity concert in Nagyszőllős in 1892. It is a sort of Hungarian *Vltava* following the course of the Danube from its source to the sea. In the third movement the river greets Hungary at Dévény — 'It is jubilant for it has come to Hungary' — and touches a sad note as it leaves the country at the Iron Gates.

This piece has been seized upon as an early example of Bartók's Hungarian nationalism, yet his music is actually more *internationalist* than it is nationalist. His interest was in what we would now call 'world music'. While Kodály worked very much to create a distinctly Hungarian style, Bartók forged a language rooted in the peasant music of *all* the nationalities of eastern Europe and beyond. His most extensive collections were of Romanian and Slovak material but he also made collecting trips to Algeria and Turkey. As a composer this work was developed in works like the *Dance Suite* (1923), a sort of kaleidoscope of peasant music styles, the String Quartets and the *Cantata Profana* (1930). In his youthful catalogue it is significant that on the page before *The Course of the Danube* is *Wallachian Piece* (dating from 1890, when he was nine): it is Bartók's first Romanian dance.

In 1894, when Bartók was thirteen, his family went to live in Pozsony (now Bratislava, the capital of Slovakia), a town with a flourishing musical life. Bartók studied with László Erkel, the son of Ferenc Erkel (1810-1893), the father of Hungarian opera and the composer of the national anthem.

Since the establishment of the Dual Monarchy in 1867 had given Hungary a sort of autonomy from Vienna, Hungarian nationalism had been at the forefront of intellectual life. An economic boom brought advances in science, technology and the arts, which were demonstrated at the huge Hungarian Millenial celebrations in 1896 commemorating the arrival of the Magyar people in the Carpathian basin a thousand years before. It was a time of unprecedented and self-conscious striving for national identity. Recent years in Budapest have seen a similar renaissance of national feeling with the return of Bartók's body to its homeland in July 1988 and the reburial of Imre Nagy as a hero in June 1989. Unfortunately the economic miracle is missing but Budapest bookshops are full of photographic albums of Hungary's 'Golden Age' and souvenir editions depicting the great Millenial Exhibition.

Opened in May 1896, the Exhibition was laid out in what is now Budapest's Városliget Park. Over 14,000 objects were displayed in historical *tableaux* that ranged from the tenth to the late-nineteenth century. A millenial village was constructed to demonstrate regional and ethnic architecture and peasants in folk costumes danced to emphasize the diversity of the country's rural traditions. A replica of the castle of János Hunyadi (Hungary's great military leader against the Turks) was built and stands in Városliget to this day.

Many of Budapest's most distinctive buildings date from this period: the Parliament, the Opera House, the Fishermen's Bastion and the underground railway (the first in continental Europe) which runs from the centre of the city to the Exhibition ground. In the visual arts, painters like Mihály Munkácsy (whose huge painting of the Magyar conquest decorates the Parliament) and the artists of the Nagybánya and Gödöllő colonies consciously tried to develop national themes. French Impressionism, *art*

Bartók on his last trip to Turkey collecting folksongs in November 1936. (photo: Collection Ferenc Bónis, Budapest)

nouveau and the landscape and folk art of Transylvania inspired the work of Károly Ferenczy and Aladár Körösfői Kriesch, who decorated the Academy of Music in Budapest. Amongst architects, Ödön Lechner drew inspiration from the vernacular styles of Transylvania and Károly Kós based his work on village churches and peasant cottages.

Folk art was seen to be the primary source of Hungarian identity. Throughout the country, centres of cottage industry were established and peasant art was revived. In the Transylvanian region of Kalotaszeg the peasants were encouraged to cultivate the local style of embroidery; it was exhibited in Budapest and soon received recognition round the world. They still sell their work to visitors.

Károly Kós began the scholarly work of collecting folk art and surveying the architecture of the Great Plain and Transylvania in expeditions that parallel the musical collecting trips of Bartók and Kodály.

When Bartók arrived in Budapest in 1899 to continue his studies at the Academy of Music, he was inevitably affected by the cultural climate. 'In music too,' he wrote, 'the aim was to create something specifically Hungarian. When this movement reached me, it drew my attention to studying Hungarian folk music, or, to be more exact, what at that time was considered folk music.' What was considered Hungarian folk music were the 'verbunkos' tunes that had accompanied recruiting ceremonies since the eighteenth century, and the songs composed by the urban gipsy orchestras. For the nationalist composers this was the Hungarian style. Liszt's Hungarian Rhapsodies were based on

15

these popular melodies while Erkel's operas, *Hunyadi László* (1844) and *Bánk bán* (1861), reworked them in operatic form. Bartók himself drew on them for *Kossuth* (1903), a symphonic poem depicting the 1848 revolution, a sort of Hungarian cross between Tchaikovsky's *1812* and Strauss's *Ein Heldenleben*. The piece caused a scandal because it parodied the Austrian national anthem, and Bartók cultivated the role of a nationalist *enfant terrible* dressed in Hungarian costume. Similar 'folk' material forms the basis of the Rhapsody for Piano and Orchestra (1905) and the first Suite for Orchestra (1905).

For Bartók the great folk music revelation came in 1904 when he spent the summer in a house in northern Hungary and heard the singing of a servant girl from Transylvania. He wrote down the songs as she sang them, 'all entirely unknown melodies, and more importantly, melodies which were completely different from the known urban Hungarian popular song types. This first experiment pointed the way to unlimited possibilities: I decided I would follow this path.' Around this time he became acquainted with Zoltán Kodály, who had also become interested in Hungarian folksong, and they started to make collecting trips. Bartók's first major expedition was to the south of Hungary in 1906 when he went equipped with knapsack and phonograph, and their first peasant song collection was published at the end of the year. He wrote some notes on collecting in 1936:

> As a general rule, women know more songs and sing in a more trustworthy way than men. Different reasons may account for this circumstance: men travel more, the character of the work they do is not as conducive to singing and they have less appreciation for music —the tunes are considered to be frivolities. Contrary to public belief, greater opportunity to frequent taverns is not paralleled by greater music appreciation.
>
> If, after lengthy persuasion, the performer begins to sing, he very often begins with an unfitting song. In such a case, so as to bolster his ego, it is advisable to pretend to take notes; perhaps later on something more suitable will turn up. A little trick such as this often can be very helpful to the collector.
>
> But however skilful or cunning we are, successful collecting — just the same as hunting — still depends very often on a stroke of chance whether a good catch will appear before the phonograph. For our precious old songs are teetering on the brink of disappearance!

Bartók and Kodály's luckiest catch was made on a trip to Transylvania in 1907 following in the footsteps of the visual artists in search of folkloristic inspiration. Amongst the Székelys, an ethnic group of Hungarians living in the eastern Carpathians, they heard a great many ancient pentatonic melodies which, they suspected, were a relic of what the Magyars had brought with them on their migration from their homeland on the Asiatic steppes. Just as the artists combined folk motifs with influences from French Impressionism and *art nouveau*, Bartók found an affinity between age-old folk music and modern musical thought.

> I became acquainted with Debussy's work, studied it thoroughly, and was greatly surprised to find in his work 'pentatonic phrases' similar in character to those contained in our peasant music. I was sure these could be attributed to influences of folk music from Eastern Europe, very likely from Russia. Similar influences can be traced in Igor Stravinsky's work. It seems therefore that, in our age, modern music

Bartók collecting folksongs from Slovak peasants in the village of Darzas, 1907. (photo: Collection Ferenc Bónis, Budapest)

has developed along similar lines in countries geographically far apart. It has become rejuvenated under the influence of a kind of peasant music that has remained untouched by the musical creations of the last centuries.

For the young Hungarian artists this became a sort of ideal — as expressed by Béla Balázs, the librettist of *Bluebeard's Castle*: 'We believed that the completely new could be transplanted only from the completely old.'

Once he had discovered the ancient layer of Hungarian music Bartók became more and more dismissive of the urban style, and musicologists have followed his lead. Yet peasant and urban music have much in common: Hungarian folksong was frequently an influence on popular songs and even in the remotest parts of the country urban songs have become part of the oral tradition and serve the function of folksongs. In their collecting both Bartók and Kodály were highly selective in their material; it was not an objective survey but a passionate trawl for what they felt was most valuable. Bartók in particular had developed a strong dislike of the urban *bourgeoisie* because they had failed to respond to his music. He, likewise, was little interested in theirs: 'The smell of the city — I loathe it! I am spending happy hours among my dear peasants.'

Just as bagpipes and haggis mean Scotland to the outside world, however, so gipsy bands and goulash represent Hungary. And some of the tunes are authentic: Brahms, in his *Hungarian Dances* (which are often cited as prime examples of gipsy-style fakery), quotes a csárdás which you can hear in the Transylvanian village of Szék to this day, even if it is a tune which slips easily into the Austro-German tradition. Bartók was interested in precisely the opposite.

17

Since 1906 Bartók had been attracted by the music of the other nationalities living in Hungary. Often they lived in more primitive conditions and preserved more valuable material, and typically he identified with them as the oppressed. His collections of Slovakian and Romanian material far outnumbered the Hungarian. By 1918, when his expeditions had to come to an end, in addition to a few Ruthenian, Bulgarian and Serbian pieces, he had collected 2,721 Hungarian, 3,000 Slovak and more than 3,500 Romanian folksongs. Even during the First World War, when nationalism grew to fever pitch, Bartók's direct contact with the peasantry and instinctive internationalism kept him apart from the frenzy. Due to ill health he was exempt from military service and was able to continue collecting in Transylvania and elsewhere. But when the war was over the dismemberment of Hungary and the nationalist preoccupations of Romania and Czechoslovakia meant that his collecting days were over. In addition, he was declared unpatriotic for publishing a study of Romanian folk music: his interest in other musical cultures was simply not understood in Budapest. Sickened by the political turmoil in Hungary he considered emigrating to Austria, Germany — or Transylvania, which had become part of Romania.

Now when these peasants are at war at the command of their leaders, and the different nationalities seem to be intent on obliterating one another, perhaps it is appropriate to point out that there is not — and never has been — the slightest trace of hatred or animosity against each other among those people. They live peacefully side by side, each speaking his own language, following his own customs, taking it for granted that his neighbour, speaking another language, does the same. An overwhelming proof of this is offered by the words of the lyric folksongs, the mirror of the people's soul. It is hard to find among these words any thought expressing animosity towards other nationalities. There is peace among the peasants; hatred against their brothers is fostered only by the higher circles!

This rich supply of peasant material provided the key to his own musical style and from 1907 it became central to his compositions. *Three Hungarian Folksongs from Csik District* (1907) were based on melodies collected amongst the Székelys in Transylvania. *For Children* (1908-9) incorporated a lot of his Slovak songs and the *Sonatina, Romanian Folkdances* and the *Romanian Christmas Carols* (all from 1915) exploited his Romanian material.

Bartók's style gradually assimilated the peasant material so that it is impossible to tell where folk melodies end and original composition begins. In the *Dance Suite* (1923) the national self-consciousness is gone and peasant-like melodies of diverse character are juxtaposed. It is a musical statement of his belief in the brotherhood of the peasants.

In his mature style Bartók went beyond folk-style melodies to a modern personal language rooted in peasant music. A sinewy, rhythmic drive derives from the dance music he had heard. The pentatonic style of the old Hungarian songs led to a new lyric and harmonic style based on fourths, and those sharp and spicy chords which are both major and minor at the same time must come from the instrumental music of Transylvania. He was fascinated by the technique of the Romanian fiddlers, and their bowing styles and quarter tones creep into his work. But all these influences are at their best in the works where the folkloristic element is not over-pronounced but balanced with a classical sense of proportion and structure. Works like the Piano Concertos, the Music for Strings, Percussion and Celesta and the Concerto for Orchestra are unthinkable without the models of Bach and Beethoven. And at the same time, the Divertimento for Strings is permeated with the sound of Transylvanian dance music, while the last movement of the String Quartet No. 4 virtually recreates the wild sounds and rhythms of the Csángó musicians from Gyimes.

*

Duke Bluebeard's Castle (1911) was Bartók's most significant work at that time to benefit from his folk music expeditions. Yet characteristically he looked out as well as in: he exploited his discoveries of Hungarian folksong but also drew on the European movements of Symbolism and Impressionism. Béla Balázs was primarily influenced by Maeterlinck's *Ariane et Barbe-Bleu*. Closely involved in the intellectual circle around Bartók and Kodály, he must have also been aware, however, of the Hungarian folk ballads on similar themes. Kodály discovered the *Ballad of Anna Molnár* among the Székelys of Transylvania and variants have been collected elsewhere. The ballad tells of a woman, Anna Molnár, who is lured away from her husband and child by a mysterious man. On their journey they sit down to rest in the shade of a tree. The man warns her not to look up into the branches but when he falls asleep Anna looks up. She sees six beautiful girls hanging in the tree. When he wakes the man asks her to climb into the branches. 'I don't know how to,' she says, 'you must show me.' So he takes off his coat and sword, and climbs the tree to demonstrate. Anna kills him, takes his horse and rides home.

Balázs intended the libretto of *Bluebeard* for Kodály, but it turned out to be Bartók who was more attracted to it. Kodály set the *Ballad of Anna Molnár* as a choral piece in 1936.

The music of *Bluebeard* demonstrates its twin sources of inspiration. On the one hand its model is *Pelléas and Mélisande*, and at the same time it is a purely Hungarian opera. The opening pages are based on the perfect fourths typical of old Hungarian songs and the vocal lines adopt their *parlando rubato* spoken rhythm. The earlier operas of Erkel, despite Hungarian subjects and national colour, had followed Italian models. The vocal lines were often quite unsuited to Hungarian words. In that sense *Bluebeard* is 100 per cent Hungarian. Its melodies have the characteristic falling pattern of Hungarian folksong and the dactylic rhythm of the language. The first syllable in Hungarian is always accented which can give translations into English a *Hiawatha* character. The influence of folksong is totally assimilated. There are no actual folk melodies but their force is used to create another world — not folkloristic but dark and mysterious. They open the way to deeper regions of the mind.

The problem with *The Wooden Prince* is that it is self-consciously folkloristic. The ballet, based on a rather limp fairy-tale by Béla Balázs, was a great success with the public when it was first produced in 1917. These 'trial of love' stories occur in some Hungarian ballads but it is thought they originate outside Hungarian territories. The most famous is *Sárighasú kigyó* (The Yellow-Bellied Snake) and tells of a young man with a poisonous snake in his jacket. He asks help to get it out but his mother and father refuse, fearing they may lose an arm in the process. The man's true love comes forward, willing to risk anything to save him. She plunges her hand into his jacket and pulls out the snake only to find that it is a bag of gold coins as a reward for her love. *The Wooden Prince* is a more arduous story of playing hard-to-get.

The score juxtaposes the human world of the Prince and Princess against the natural world of the forest. The human characters are depicted with broad folk-like melodies while their environment is painted in a more impressionistic

19

style. The work has been compared to the folk-influenced *art nouveau* produced in Hungary around the same time.

The ballet begins with a beautiful passage evoking the force of nature. Bartók slowly builds up a richly consonant C major chord which echoes the portrayal of the unspoilt Rhine at the start of Wagner's *Ring*. The folk-like melodies appear with the dance of the Princess in the forest and the departure of the Prince. Whereas the short motifs and fragments Bartók used in *Bluebeard* could be assimilated into a symphonic form, here, because he is using complete folk-like melodies, they feel less integrated into the musical language. Typically Bartók writes a grotesque variation on the Prince's melody for the Wooden Prince and then goes to town with folk-style dances with rough parallel chords. But the most beautiful moment in *The Wooden Prince* is when the saxophones enter with a pentatonic melody which suggests nothing so much as the sound of the reedy 'taragot' playing on a hillside in the open air. And if the ballet has any power it is as a statement about the purity of the open air and nature. Just as Bartók's openness to 'world music' has now become fashionable, his views on the destruction of the environment have come into their own. For him folk music was part of the fascinating richness of the natural world:

> Peasant music, in the strict sense of the word, must be regarded as a natural phenomenon. It is just as much a natural phenomenon as, for instance, the various manifestations of Nature in fauna and flora.

Bartók's last stage work, *The Miraculous Mandarin*, is a depiction of the violent and corrupting world of Man. It is the antithesis of the *Cantata Profana* written a decade later as a hymn to the purity of folksong and village life. This unmistakably urban subject opens with car horns and the roar of the metropolis. The music is sometimes as graphic as a comic-strip. There is nothing like a folksong (the Mandarin's pentatonic tune is oriental rather than Magyar), yet paradoxically the impact of peasant music is audible in almost every bar. And, whereas *Bluebeard* and *The Wooden Prince* are essentially Hungarian in character, *The Miraculous Mandarin* is a synthesis of all the peasant music Bartók had heard on his travels into a distinctive language of his own. It is 'world music' abstracted from any geographical location and wrought into a taut symphonic form. The rhythm of the dances, the modal patterns of the songs and the harmonies and quarter tones of the peasant fiddlers are all there, although distorted and fragmented in Bartók's expressionist urban nightmare. This is rural music recomposed to depict the alienation of the city.

Sadly the inferno of the *Mandarin* can be seen to mirror Bartók's situation at the time. The First World War held grim prospects for Hungary. It is not hard to hear the horrors of war in the score. At the same time as he was writing the brutal opening bars of *The Miraculous Mandarin* he was setting some of the most beautiful songs he had collected in Transylvania. These were the last simple settings of folksongs that Bartók wrote.

Set design by Desző Zádor for the first Budapest production, 1918. (photo: Collection Ferenc Bónis, Budapest)

The 1936 Hungarian State Opera production designed by Gusztáv Oláh seen here with Mihály Székely as Bluebeard and Ella Némethy as Judith. (photo: Collection Ferenc Bónis, Budapest)

Elizabeth Laurence as Judith in Leslie McGahey's 1989 BBC Television production (photo: BBC)

Annie Miller

'The Ballad of Anna Molnár', as sung by Samu Szabó, Transylvania 1872
translated by Peter Sherwood and Keith Bosley

Come with me, Annie Miller
come, let us hide away.
I will not go with you, sir knight:
I have a little boy
who gives me not a moment's rest
by night nor yet by day.

Oh come, come, Annie Miller:
I have six mansions fair
and in the seventh you shall dwell.
So he persuaded her.

Far, far away they travelled
to a leafy forest glade.
Sit down here, Annie Miller
within this green tree's shade
and let me lie upon your lap
while you shall groom my head.

But beware, Annie Miller:
into the tree don't peep!
I will not peep, sir knight, she said
and sir knight he fell asleep.

Then Annie Miller she looked up
she peeped into the tree:
six pretty maids were hanging there.
A seventh he'll make me!

Her tender heart began to pound
and her warm tears to drop:
they dropped apace upon his face
and woke sir knight right up.

Why, Annie Miller, do you weep?
You peeped into the tree!
But I did not look up, sir knight:
three orphans just went by —

and I was minded of my son
kind sir, my little boy
who gave me not a moment's rest
by night nor yet by day.

You go first, Annie Miller
up into the green tree.
I'll not go first, sir knight: I'm used
to someone ahead of me.

So sir knight ahead he went instead
and as he turned his back
she snatched away his flashing sword
and whacked the head off his neck.

She put his clothes on, his red coat
that reached down to the ground
leapt on his stead and home did speed
to the gates of her kind husband.

Goodman, kind goodman, can you spare
a bed where I may lie?
I cannot spare a bed, sir knight:
I have a little boy
who gives me not a moment's rest
by night nor yet by day.

Goodman, kind goodman, I am
well used to such a thing.
Is there some good wine hereabouts?
There is, and not far to bring.

Kind goodman, to the table
go bring a jugful straight
and go bring too, good servant
some kindling for the fire.

Her clothes she unbuttoned, her red coat
that reached down to the ground
and gave suck to her little boy
who soon was sleeping sound.

Home came the kindly goodman.
Sir knight, sir knight, said he
my little boy is sleeping —
and yet how can this be?
For three weeks and three days now
he has not shut an eye.

Goodman, kind goodman, tell me:
if your wife came this way
would you then beat her, scold her
until her dying day?
No, I'd not beat nor scold her
until her dying day.

Her clothes she unbuttoned, her red coat
that reached down to the ground
and now she kissed her little boy —
her son, her kind husband.

Don Garrard as Bluebeard, Sadler's Wells Opera, 1972. (photo: Reg Wilson)

A Foot in Bluebeard's Door

Julian Grant

'Nothing is likely about masterpieces,' wrote Stravinsky, 'least of all whether there will be any.' Of no opera is this more true than Bartók's *Bluebeard*, an opera from a composer with no previous experience of the theatre and from a country with, at best, a tenuous tradition of opera and concert music. From the end of the eighteenth century, music with a Hungarian tinge swept Europe, imitated by salon composers and figures of the calibre of Haydn, Brahms and Liszt. This was a highly romanticised idiom based on the flamboyant music of travelling gipsies (Bartók called it 'gipsy slop'), not the authentic voice of the peasant that Bartók and Kodály later collected, and which Liszt had mistakenly assumed was of no value. One composer, Ferenc Erkel (1810-93), wrote *Hunyadi László* (1844) and *Bánk bán* (1861), nationalist operas of French and Italian derivation with Hungarian accretions. Erkel remained unique, however, spawning no tradition comparable to Glinka in Russia or Skroup and Smetana in Czechoslovakia. Just as in England, nationalism in music flowered late in Hungary. Vaughan-Williams and Bartók both collected folksong when cultural traditions were disappearing and a world war was destroying the environment where folksong could flourish. As Bartók said, 'I had the great privilege to be a close observer of an as yet homogeneous, but unfortunately rapidly disappearing, social structure expressing itself in music.'

But nationalism is only part of the soil whence *Duke Bluebeard's Castle* sprang, and an outline of Bartók's career until its completion in 1911 is instructive, because *Bluebeard* can be seen as the first major work where all the influences on him meld together. His first completed orchestral work, *Kossuth*, dates from 1903. It is a symphonic poem depicting the life and death of László Kossuth, hero of the Hungarian war of Independence in 1848. Ironically, this great patriotic success is voiced with a strong German accent — that of Richard Strauss — whose *Also Sprach Zarathustra* received its Budapest première in 1902, arousing Bartók to compose 'as by a lightning stroke'. Strauss's influence was dominant until the summer of 1906, when Bartók made his first extensive folksong collecting tour. In the following years he became better known as a folklorist than as a composer, arranging many songs for concert use, while his piano bagatelles of this period begin to show traces of folk inflections. The first String Quartet (1907), over which Bartók laboured for an entire year, shows a command of motivic and contrapuntal writing couched in a folk idiom that is well on the way to being as personal as that in *Bluebeard*. Kodály provided the last major formative influence by bringing scores from Paris in 1908, putting Bartók within the orbit of Debussy. Further orchestral works, *Two Portraits* (1908), *Two Pictures* (1910) and *Four Pieces* (1912), show the colourful and opulent way in which his orchestral imagination developed, at first imitating the French composer and then going beyond him. Thus, Bartók evolved a contemporary language rooted in authentic national sources and free from the shadow of German musical culture that had dominated Hungarian music for so long.

Béla Balázs wrote concerning his *Bluebeard* text: 'I wanted to magnify the dramatic fluidity of the Székely folk ballads for the stage. And I wanted to depict a modern soul in the primary colours of folksong' — a statement that also sums up Bartók's intentions in this piece and shows the closeness of expressive aim of librettist and composer. Bartók did not attempt to outline the structural formality of the text in a musical way, no doubt sensing a danger of monotony in a work where the opening of seven doors is the only action. Although the loose tonal scheme mirrors Balázs' arch form, the action is controlled with an acute sense of timing and psychological insight into the two protagonists so that the doors, for all their extravagant musical depiction, become a logical extension of their relationship. Bartók's word-setting is equally varied. In homage to Hungarian folk ballads, Balázs wrote throughout in eight-syllable lines and it is a fortunate legacy of Bartók's systematic work on the linguistic elements of folksong that he knew how to avoid oppressive symmetry. He was certainly alive to the use of repetition in the libretto, whether for enigmatic, emphatic or atmospheric reasons, a device which shows Balázs to have been a true disciple of Maeterlinck, the Belgian symbolist playwright. Correspondingly there is much direct repetition of one or two bar units in the score, which has a precedent in folk music to be sure, but is also a strong feature of Debussy's music, where it is an all-pervasive tic. This feature appears far less in Bartók's later works. *Bluebeard* is a descendant of *Pelléas et Mélisande* by Debussy and Maeterlinck (1902) in its fidelity to the naturalistic stresses of language, though the often monotonal setting of French in *Pelléas* obviously contrasts with the more sing-song inflections of Hungarian.

The libretto can be said to outline an arch, with a story beginning and ending in darkness and reaching its brightest point at the centre (the opening of the fifth door), and the music pays lip service to this in a tonal scheme, starting in F#, reaching C major in the centre and returning to F# at the close. Within this there is a continual progression — as C is the halfway point in the scale between the poles of F#, the work passes through D#/Eb (the second and fourth doors), past C to A (sixth door) and on to the end, outlining a diminished seventh, though it is typical of Bartók's approach that these stages are not too emphatic. More significantly, the area of F# is associated with Bluebeard and the enclosed world of his domain, and C with the world outside: with brightness, with Judith and with the appearance of the former wives. The tritone interval F#-C, known in old musical treatises as the 'diabolus in musica', because it is dissonant and lacks tonality, permeates the score. Used melodically it is a feature of the Lydian mode, a favourite of Bartók and a commonplace in Central European folk music.

Just how far Bartók had come from Germanic tradition is shown by the almost complete absence of leitmotifs. The one exception is a simple interval [7] of a minor second, that appears initially wherever Judith discovers blood, and later stains the score with wider expressive meaning. Otherwise Bartók rejected Wagner's method of score-building, which had spread to Italy, Russia and France (even Debussy's *Pelléas*), for something more indigenous, a subtle motivic transformation derived from Liszt's pioneering techniques of thematic metamorphosis. In *Bluebeard*, this attained a flexibility which points the way to the intellectual concision of his later masterpieces.

Through his technical fluency Bartók was able to skirt the crisis that affected music in the years immediately preceding World War One. Broadly speaking, the Western musical system of major and minor keys had become so enriched with chromaticism, modality and new harmonic discoveries that the rules of tonal harmony were no longer relevant. Schönberg and his pupils proclaimed the death of tonality and abandoned it but the impact of their revolution came later, when their works were more widely performed. At the time, Strauss was seen as the leader of the avant-garde and in 1909 *Elektra*, a

Katalin Mészöly and György Melis in a production directed by András Mikó at the Erkel Theatre, Budapest to celebrate the centenary of Bartók's birth in 1981. (photo: Hulton-Deutsche Collection)

work Bartók admired greatly, seemed the high watermark of modernism. But in *Elektra* a distinct stylistic chasm appears between the lyrical music, grounded in nineteenth-century romanticism, and other passages of expressionist angst couched in a language that embraces atonality. Significantly, Strauss retreated in his next work, *Der Rosenkavalier*, and many followed suit by staging strategic retreats in the inter-war years; composers of the calibre of Stravinsky and Debussy — and (two decades later) Copland and Prokofiev. Bartók, however, assimilated ideas from Schönberg to Stravinsky and neo-classicism, without feeling the need of an abrupt stylistic volte-face. So ingrained was his use of folk material, and the language he minted so flexible, that even in an early work like *Bluebeard* he could encompass extremes without sacrificing unity of style. In the final scene of the opera, for instance, the music becomes extremely strenuous and dissonant, but Bartók can revert to his opening material with no feeling of disunity.

Nevertheless, there was a tendency among composers of the period to use external elements as an alternative organizing agent to tonality, and an equation of music with colour is a fleeting, though fascinating, preoccupation. It plays a part in Balázs' and Bartók's scheme for *Bluebeard*: the first four doors are accompanied by stage instructions specifying the projection of colours. Previous composers, notably Rimsky-Korsakov and Scriabin, had associated keys and harmonies with specific colours; Schönberg in his correspondence with Kandinsky and in *Die glückliche Hand* (1908-13) — a contemporary work of *Bluebeard* and Scriabin's *Prometheus* (with its part for an invented colour-organ) — took the relationship further. Bartók was not so rigorous, though the music for the doors is far more static harmonically than the surrounding music for Judith and Bluebeard. This makes a sole point of contact with another Maeterlinck opera, *Ariane et Barbe-Bleue* (1907) by Paul Dukas, a feminist version of the legend that Balázs knew, though Bartók makes no reference to it. In the Dukas, the opening of the doors reveals jewels of different colours, depicted in washes of gorgeously orchestrated static harmony — serving a similar function to the Bartók in bringing stability to an unstable harmonic language. Perhaps both composers have a common source in Wagner, whose great depictions, not of colour, but of nature, feature long periods where harmonic motion is suspended — the start of *The Rhinegold*, and forest-murmurs in *Siegfried* above all — that are now seen as precursors of musical impressionism. That Bartók had not totally exorcised his spectre is shown strongly at the opening of *The Wooden Prince*, with over 60 bars of Lydian C major reminiscent of the opening of *The Rhinegold*. Apart from some references in *The Miraculous Mandarin*, colour as an external element plays no further part in Bartók's work.

Colour, in an orchestral sense, is another matter. Bartók employed a large orchestra (four each of flutes, bassoons, horns, trumpets and trombones; three oboes and clarinets; two harps; celesta) including a full organ and four extra onstage trumpets and trombones. These forces are used with great restraint, some shattering climaxes aside, more in the manner of Debussy's *Pelléas* than the sophisticated timbral cocktail of Strauss's *Salome*. The feats of orchestral virtuosity are reserved for the opening of the doors which, as mentioned before, tend to be less motivic and more overtly coloristic; otherwise, Bartók's use of the orchestra is very economical and unerring in its control of atmosphere. For all his admiration of Debussy, so evident from the harp *glissandi* and divided strings of the orchestral *Portraits* and *Pictures*, the sound world of *Bluebeard* has a sharpness which keeps the strands of orchestral colour separate; and this propensity for primary colours is more akin to Liszt and the Russian Nationalists.

*

The opening music depicts Bluebeard's domain with a pentatonic string phrase in F♯ [1]; and a disruption of this pure state is immediately apparent in a woodwind phrase nervously centering on C [2]. The opposition of the two protagonists is further emphasised by their first words, a simple modal line for Bluebeard [3] and something more chromatic and insinuating for Judith [4]. Her music is here tenuously related to F♯, assuming the tonality of Bluebeard's castle, her new home; and her answers to Bluebeard's repeated questions whether she regrets abandoning her family are unequivocal [5]. The door by which they entered shuts behind them, and Judith gropes her way forward in the darkness to a lower string *ostinato*, related to the very opening [6], which evolves, throwing out related shoots, a folky phrase for Judith recounting the rumours surrounding Bluebeard and a rocking clarinet motif. As Judith feels the walls sweating, the blood motif [7] makes its first appearance, and further explorations extend the clarinet motif [8]. Judith maintains that she will never miss the daylight and evades Bluebeard's questions; when he asks, 'Tell me why you came here' to a pause in the *ostinato*, she responds by stating that she will dry and warm the stone, and the *ostinato* splutters, taken over by the clarinet motif that builds and switches between the areas of F♯ and C. She notices the seven doors and insists they are opened [9] to a variant of the rocking motif [8], which graphically depicts her hammering on the first door. Her determination is dampened when the answer is '. . . a cavernous sigh, like night winds sighing down long, dismal corridors' [10] —

this phrase slides the tonality from the locality of C to a firm F# and a varied repetition of the opening [1] overlaid with an uneasy clarinet line. She weeps as she hears the castle groan. This skilful passage delays the inevitable opening of the first door. Bartók's sense of pace is very telling, as is his manipulation of Judith's state of mind when she recovers from her shock and fear (a viola phrase [11]), masters herself and applies emotional blackmail [12]: 'open together . . . open because I love you'. Judith sings this to a lulling, expressive phrase, but a clarinet, flickering with barely repressed anxiety, clashes with her vocal line by a semitone, undermining her soothing words and reminding us of her purpose.

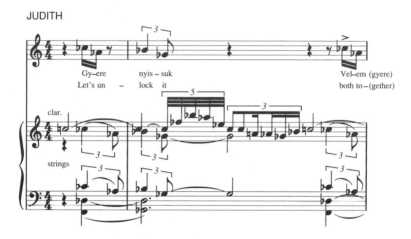

Once the key is in her hand, the coaxing stops, the muted string textures vanish and are replaced by a clearer woodwind sound with obsessive flicker, graphically depicting her steely determination.

The first door opens to reveal Bluebeard's torture chamber in a beam of red light. A minor second tremolo (the blood motif), later changed to a trill, colours the whole passage, with vivid woodwind and xylophone flourishes outlining a tritone [13]. The sharpness of the orchestral palette is all the more effective for the preceding restraint. Trumpets state the blood motif [7], with a swaggering Magyar melody on clarinets [14a] as Judith recoils in horror from the bleeding walls. Immediately she turns her back to it and, silhouetted against the red light, equates it with a sunrise; resolutely she summons up her courage to the same melody, hectically speeded up and brightened in the strings [14b]. She demands the other keys, and the music reaches a searing climax with the words:

BLUEBEARD: Judith, tell me why you want to.
JUDITH: I love you.

Here all the musical elements combine — the trill, the blood motif and the swaggering melody [14a] turned into an emotional threnody, a lament for the inability of these two lovers to be of one mind. This subsides, leaving only the trill while Bluebeard grants permission to open the next door — a distant echo of the persistent trill which accompanies Salome's depraved kiss in Strauss's opera.

The second door shows Bluebeard's armoury in a reddish-yellow light, to martial flourishes for small clarinets, oboes and trumpets [15a]. Almost immediately Judith sees blood [7] and wishes to know more, demanding more keys. Walking back, she describes the light to a beautiful variant of the trumpet fanfare [15b] with a heartfelt folk flavour and a lush major-minor modality that is almost bluesy. Her badgering becomes more aggressive with a fleeting reminiscence of Kundry, Wagner's manipulative siren in *Parsifal*.

Bartók

Wagner

Bluebeard, in an *arioso* passage of great expressive power, grants Judith three more keys but bids her not to ask him any more questions [16]. Door three reveals his treasury in a gold light, a pure stream of D major luminously scored for cello and viola harmonics, three muted trumpets and fluttertongue flutes, over which violins float gently dissonant arabesques [17]. When Judith notices the blood, Bluebeard hurries her on to the next door. This opens onto a garden in a blue-green light, depicted in another wash of static harmony based in Eb, a web of divided strings through which emerge a horn call and clarinet answer [18], soon transformed into a characteristic syncopated idea followed by a sweeping gesture in plain Ab major, that seems to transport us out of doors [19]. To this last theme Judith sings of the beauty of the flowers and Bluebeard dubs her the crowning glory of his garden, and it is then immediately repeated, grindingly dissonant, as Judith discovers that blood has stained a white rose. Again comes the blood motif [7] and Bluebeard swiftly urges Judith on to the fifth door.

Now, with a blinding light, a massive C major theme thunders out [20] on full orchestra with extra brass and organ, capped by Judith's top C exclamation. The physical impact of the reinforced orchestration and the brightly scored chains of (exclusively) major triads ensure the overwhelming effect of this celebrated passage in performance. This is intensified by an almost hysterical sense of release; cunningly, Bartók has emphasized G, the dominant of C, in the lead up to the climax, and this dominant preparation with characteristic added dissonances, resolves as expected, acting as a perverse surprise in a work that thrives on more equivocal harmonic relationships. C major has traditionally been associated with light and purity by many composers but the two sources closest to Bartók, and similarly

Henk Smit and Katherine Ciesinski in Herbert Wernicke's production for the Netherlands Opera, 1988. (photo: Jaap Pieper)

engulfing in mood, are the spectacular sunrise at the opening of *Also Sprach Zarathustra* and Brünnhilde's awakening and the final duet of *Siegfried*. Incidentally, Bartók specifies a soprano for Judith's role, but it is often performed by a mezzo-soprano, as the forays into the top register are few and much of the writing favours the middle and low registers.

Bluebeard shows the vast extent of his realm to a triumphant phrase [21a]; Judith replies abstractedly, all animation gone, in Bluebeard's 'inner' tonality of F# (here notated enharmonically in G♭), destroying any finality the emphatic C major implied [21b]. Although she notices blood here as well, Bluebeard ignores her anxiety and asks her to kiss him to a lumbering pair of themes in C major [22]: in his mind no more doors will be opened, the progress is finished. Judith, however, repeatedly asks for the remaining keys, eroding the bright C major, turning Bluebeard's exhilaration to bleak resignation. An agitated passage, obsessively centering upon the 'blood' interval, a minor second [23] underlines Judith's inexorable demands. Bluebeard warns her to take care but crumples to a *presto* passage that lead to inarticulate hammer blows on four kettledrums, low woodwind and strings. The castle groans again, to a telescoped gesture derived from [10], the light from the previous doors dims and Judith perceives a lake of tears, portrayed by Bartók with infinite orchestral subtlety; a contained *arpeggio* figure in A with a hint of the blood motif in a clashing semitone at the top, blurred and disguised by varied figuration on harps, celesta, flute and clarinet.

Adagio

Judith's plangent four-note phrase based on C [24a] is repeated four times, and each harmonisation increases in intensity until it clashes directly, inhabiting F#, Bluebeard's domain, while a sombre string passage adds to the mood of stillness and depression [24b]. Bluebeard vows that the last door will remain closed forever, and to this Judith appears to concede, exhorting him to kiss her; two major chords provide huge — but shortlived — relief from the surrounding tortuous harmonies. An impassioned modal theme [25] erupts over a chordal base that becomes increasingly strained and bitonal. It is a passage that is not marked in the libretto, and is part of Bartók's scheme to emphasize the depth of this relationship. Judith imagines that she has guessed what lies beyond the seventh door, and requests its opening in a circuitous way, asking Bluebeard about her predecessors to a slow insistent theme permeated with the blood motif and crabbed chromatic intervals [26]. Bluebeard tells her to ask no questions [25] and their two musical paragraphs alternate, in a stalemate. When she finally confronts him to open the last door, the insistent theme [26] speeds up, throwing up minor seconds in an uncontrolled expressionist outburst worthy of *Elektra*, culminating in a massive climax of [26]. Once Bluebeard has given her the final key, her delay at opening the door is eloquently voiced in a string melody [27] that is compassionate and nostalgic, as if lamenting the fact that she has violated the mystery of their love. As she puts the key in the lock, the last two doors close, leaving only the first four illuminating the scene. There are reminiscences of the theme that accompanied the sigh before the opening of the first door [10] and of the nervous woodwind flutters when Judith opened it.

The last door opens with a sudden swing to C minor, a sepulchral passage for clarinet and cor-anglais [28]. Judith is astounded to find the three former wives still living. Bluebeard introduces them in an ardent *arioso*, as his brides of the morning, noon and evening [29a], punctuated by a surging string theme [29b]. His animation contrasts strongly with Judith's collapse of will; she only mutters that she cannot compare to them. He proclaims her his bride of the night. Slowly she follows the wives beyond the door, as the music becomes ever more anguished and dissonant, culminating in a wrenching climax to a theme that irons out the blood motif and states it melodically [30], with a prominent organ part. Darkness descends, the opening theme reappears in F♯ [1], with the initial woodwind phrase, on oboes [2] finally heard on clarinets centering on C:

a nagging presence till the end, forever part of Bluebeard's memory. The opera has come full circle and yet cannot be resolved.

The opera has a reputation for being difficult to stage and appears often in concert and is frequently recorded, suiting the latter format particularly, where the mind's eye can envisage its own theatre. Kodály wrote:

> Only impenitent pedants can go on asking themselves whether this is really an opera or not. What does it matter? Call it a 'scenic symphony' or a 'drama accompanied by a symphony'. What matters is that it is impossible to separate the music and the drama and that here we have a masterpiece, a musical volcano that erupts for 60 minutes of

compressed tragedy and leaves us with only one desire: the desire to hear it again.

There is a dichotomy between the symbolist devices of colour and spectacle used in a very non-specific way and the relentless penetration of the music that turns Balázs' puppets into plausible characters. Bartók explores a psychological core at the heart of this powerful myth and gives a universality that demands a visual and dramatic complement — in short a stage, but perhaps one whose source is found through the probings of the music, not by reference to the rather dated stage directions.

It would seem that the initial rejection and seven-year delay of the première of *Bluebeard's Castle*, and the later censorship of *The Miraculous Mandarin*, inhibited Bartók from further stage work. Given the skill shown in this score, one can only regret that, like Shostakovich, a potentially great opera composer of our century was derailed by external events.

Amsterdam's 1988 production designed and directed by Herbert Wernicke with Katherine Ciesinski and Henk Smit. (photo: Jaap Pieper)

Around the Bluebeard Myth

Mike Ashman

The Bluebeard story first achieved widespread dissemination in the *Histoires ou Contes du temps passé* (1697) of the French poet and critic Charles Perrault. These *Contes* established a canon of European 'folk' or 'fairy' tales, many of which may now be seen to be related — *Beauty and the Beast* and *Bluebeard* are associated by Bruno Bettelheim as variants of the 'animal-groom cycle' in which 'for love, a radical change in previously held attitudes about sex is absolutely necessary. What must happen is expressed, as always in fairy tales, through a most impressive image: a beast is turned into a magnificent person.' Perrault called his bridegroom 'La Barbe Bleue' (the Bluebeard). Perhaps he was aware of mythological precedents — the beards of Bes, Indra and Zeus were blue and, in legends of the battle of Darkness and Light, a blue beard signifies the blue-blackness of night. He has been criticised both for fabricating a folktale which had little or no oral tradition, and for passing off history as legend. All the elements of the Bluebeard myth were, however, in place before he published the *Contes*.

In *Genesis II* and *III*, God plays Bluebeard (and the serpent, perhaps, the key) in an account of a broken taboo. Eve tastes the fruit of 'the tree of the knowledge of good and evil' despite the warning that she will die if she does so. Perrault's first moral from *La Barbe Bleue* was that 'curiosity despite all its attractions often costs us much regret'. While the Biblical story warns against the danger of inquisitiveness, Eve's action is implicitly necessary in the quest for knowledge and the subsequent history of humankind. This theme is present in the classical myth of Cupid and Psyche, in which Psyche's curiosity to know the identity of her lover compelled her to steal a look at him while he slept; awoken by a drop of oil from her lamp, he disappeared, and the lovers were only reunited after Psyche had undergone numerous trials from Aphrodite. The motif of a forbidden action or question occurs elsewhere in Greek mythology, for instance in the myth of Semele and Zeus. It probably originated in a superstition that anonymity brought strength, but it soon became associated with male feelings of superiority, in which the woman learns too late that her patience would have been rewarded by full knowledge. And other Greek myths can be connected to Bluebeard. The tale of Helen, rescued by her brothers after she had been kidnapped by Theseus, for instance, is a topos for the family rescue of a bride-to-be who has disappeared. That of Pandora's box parallels the Garden of Eden story in which the 'fall' of man is blamed upon the woman: Pandora broke her promise to her new husband not to open a box, and in so doing she released 'all the Spites that might plague mankind'.[1] History would not have been the same without her.

Medieval sources added further to the legend. In the anonymous epic *Lohengrin*, there is a bridegroom/saviour (also mentioned in Eschenbach's *Parzival*) whose provenance must not be questioned. The fourteenth-century romance of *Perceforest* tells of a physical transformation — the blackening of a finger, then a hand — when forbidden physical contact is made. The first hint at the motiveless evil of Perrault's bridegroom occurs in this period: a Breton legend tells of a king Comorre who murdered many women, and finally his wife Tryphime; she was restored to life by St Gildas. And from Brittany also comes the identification of Bluebeard with the historical Marshal Gilles de

Rais (1404-40). After heroic exploits in the Hundred Years War at the side of Joan of Arc, Gilles de Rais withdrew to his estates, where he indulged in satanism, alchemy, and the abduction, sexual harrassment and murder of (mostly male) children — for which he was burned at the stake. De Rais' sheer excess and the volte-face from association with a saint to allegiance to Satan were powerful contributions to the construction of a legend. In the nineteenth century, Eugène Bossard's biography of de Rais became a central text for the Symbolists; the apparently historical account reported a local legend in which an abducted woman turned into a blue devil in the course of a perverse wedding ceremony and demanded the soul of the red-bearded Marshal if he truly wished to serve the black arts. It appears, however, that the historical figure had little interest in adult women.

During the Middle Ages, tales from the Middle East and the Orient reached Europe, including several in which a despotic ruler, the victim of some sexual deception, takes revenge upon innocent subjects. Best known today are the *Turandot* fable and the cornucopia of *The Tales of the Thousand and One Nights*, where the frame story is the cunning of the latest wife (Scheherezade) to delay her execution by telling stories to the blood-thirsty Caliph. Her *Tale of the Third Calendar* concerns a misfortune consequent on the entry of a forbidden chamber through a golden door, and the gaining of wisdom through the loss of an eye.

Whether or not he was aware of these antecedents, Perrault would have known three strands of a Bluebeard myth which were current in France. The 1697 *La Barbe-Bleue* combines the vengeful wife-slaying husband, the taboo action or question and the woman's redemptive quest. Balancing these elements has provided a strong dynamic for later reworkings of the story. Variants occur in the folktale collections of the Germans Jakob and Wilhelm Grimm (1812-14, revised 1819) and Ludwig Bechstein (1857) and the Norwegians Peter Christen Asbjørnsen and Jorgen Møe (1843-44, revised 1852). Roughly contemporaneous versions were established and published in Britain, Ireland, Italy, Spain, Switzerland, Romania, Russia, North Africa and North America.

The British *Mr Fox*, the wonderfully named *Captain Murderer* (as recounted by Dickens in *The Uncommercial Traveller*) and the Grimms' *Der Räuberbräutigam* (*The Robber Bridegroom*) all stress the violent, even cannibalistic crimes of the man (or animal), and the cunning precautions taken by a woman who has managed to observe the fate of her predecessors. All end abruptly with the execution of the Bluebeard. The Romanian *The Enchanted Pig* and the Norwegian *East of the Sun and West of the Moon* rework the Cupid and Psyche myth: the man is a bewitched animal bridegroom and the woman's quest is to re-discover and 'free' her husband after she has been malevolently advised to be inquisitive about his first mysterious appearance. In the first edition of their *Kinder- und Hausmärchen* the Grimms included a *Blaubart* that was little more than a translation of Perrault. This was replaced by *Fitchers Vogel* (Fitcher's Bird), one of the few Bluebeard variants in which the woman successfully deludes the man into thinking that she has not entered the forbidden room. His giant's power is broken and he is made to serve the woman (transporting her resurrected sisters back home) before being killed by other members of her family.

Richard Wagner was in many respects as obsessive a student of folklore as the Grimms. His reworking in the 1840s of the medieval *Lohengrin* saga coincided with widespread interest in 'literary' folktales. The libretto for his 'romantic opera' includes many elements of the Bluebeard mythology. Here is

Sadler's Wells Opera's 1972 production with Ava June and Don Garrard. (photo: Reg Wilson)

the bridegroom of mysterious, quasi-divine origin; the forbidden question[2]; the deceitful encouragement of a bride to break this taboo; the question asked in a bridal chamber, followed by bloodshed; and the delayed resolution involving the breaking of a spell on a close relation (the bride's brother) previously believed dead. Wagner cited the legend of Zeus and Semele as the starting point for this proto-Bluebeard opera; it was an obvious influence on the later work of Bartók and Balázs.

From the end of the eighteenth century the Bluebeard material attracted increasingly freer adaptation by both writers and composers. Michel-Jean Sedaine (1719-97) wrote the first full-length Bluebeard opera libretto for Grétry. *Raoul Barbe-Bleue* (1789), like a 1791 setting by Dalyrac, located the story neatly in a favourite contemporary genre, the 'rescue' opera. The early German romantic Ludwig Tieck wrote both a five-act fairy tale (*Der Blaubart*, 1796) and an 'Arabesk' (or fantasy Novelle) *Die Sieben Weiber des Blaubarts* (published in 1828). In Britain memories of the story were touched in Charlotte Bronte's *Jane Eyre* — the room where Rochester has kept his demented first wife and where she burns to death — and even indirectly in *Alice in Wonderland* with its keys to mysterious doors.

By 1866 the story was ready for burlesque. Meilhac and Halévy's libretto for Offenbach makes some predictable but neat jokes — the wives are not really dead but have come to an 'arrangement' with Bluebeard's alchemist; the King who attempts to bring Bluebeard to justice is also accused of the murder of a young woman. More interesting is the librettists' awareness of the presence of Gilles de Rais in the Bluebeard story (the feudal setting, the alchemist as a pastiche of de Rais' accomplices in magic), perhaps reflecting growing contemporary interest in that angle.

The Bluebeard material's highly-coloured brew of sex, violent death, gloom and mystical self-analysis was a perfect vehicle for Symbolist treatment.

Fascination with sado-masochistic aspects of Catholic imagery and the occult led the 'Decadent' writer Joris-Karl Huysmans into a detailed study of Gilles de Rais and contact with French black magic circles. The literary result was *Là-Bas* (Down There), a thinly-disguised autobiographical journal of the researches of the writer 'Durtal' into the 'Bluebeard' part of de Rais' career. *Là-Bas* (1891) is not a Bluebeard adaptation but an important (and lurid) step in awakening Symbolist interest in the struggle between 'deep and sinful' Night and its 'beloved' enemy Light.

This metaphor is ever-present in Maurice Maeterlinck's *Ariane et Barbe-Bleue*, 1901, which enshrines a sharp, practical awareness of the history of the Bluebeard legend. It is structured like a Greek tragedy where the major events — even the discovery of the previous wives — take place offstage; there are also a Nurse who continually questions the heroine's actions and a Chorus of peasants, whose growing discontent slyly alludes to Gilles de Rais' feudally oppressed subjects. This bride has a name, Ariane, whose Greek namesake guided Theseus out of the Minotaur's cave. The only treasure which interests her in her new home is the forbidden golden key. 'All that we are allowed to do will teach us nothing', she tells her Nurse. Hearing the voices of her 'sisters' in the forbidden room, she confronts the returning Bluebeard:

BLUEBEARD   You're throwing away the happiness I wanted you to have . . .
ARIANE   The happiness I want cannot live in the shadows.
BLUEBEARD   Renounce knowledge and I can forgive . . .
ARIANE   I will be able to forgive when I know everything.

This weakened Bluebeard can never finish a sentence, cannot punish his latest wife because he is interrupted by a popular uprising and retires to seek reinforcements. Ariane lets light into the castle (by smashing all the windows) and offers freedom to Bluebeard's five previous wives. The magic of the castle appears to prevent their escape. Bluebeard returns to fight a losing battle with the peasants. He is brought into his own castle apparently garotted to death. The castle's magic collapses. But the other wives restore him to life: the legend will not die! Ariane leaves, unable to persuade her 'sisters' to return with her to the light.

Maeterlinck's text (set by Paul Dukas in 1907) reads in part like a feminist answer to the male tyranny which has dominated the first two strands of the Bluebeard story. It is the first treatment of the story which uses Bluebeard's house as a direct metaphor for his soul and identifies his possessions with states of mind. This link was taken over directly by Balázs.[3] Maeterlinck's ending is wholly tragic rather than recuperative: the mission of Light (or knowledge) has failed. Béla Balázs' *A kékszakállú herceg vára* (Duke Bluebeard's Castle),[4] set by Bartók in 1911, is centred on the male ego. The proselytising, would-be liberator Judith — a name as closely derived from the Bible's slayer of Holofernes as Maeterlinck's heroine is from Greek myth — is, with varying degrees of willingness, actually handed the keys to the seven doors of Bluebeard's castle (and psyche). Temptation is replaced by graded invitation. At the end, as in Maeterlinck, there is only darkness — a darkness which nobody leaves and into which even Bluebeard disappears.

1. Robert Graves, *The Greek Myths*, Vol. 1. (London, 1955)
2. The Frageverbot is found in both Wagner's medieval sources.
3. Maeterlinck identifies himself with this metaphor by giving the names of heroines of his own plays to Bluebeard's previous wives.
4. A Hungarian source for Bluebeard has been noted in the *Ballad of Anna Molnár*.

Thematic Guide

Many of the themes from this opera have been identified in the articles by numbers in square brackets, which refer to the themes set out on these pages. The themes are also identified by the numbers in square brackets at the corresponding points in the libretto, so that the words can be related to the musical themes.

[1]

[2]

[3] BLUEBEARD

I – me lás–sad: ez a   kék - sza - kál - lú   vá – ra,
Here you stand a – lone with   Blue-beard and his   cas - tle,

[4] JUDITH

Meg-yek,   meg-yek, _____   Kék – sza kál – lú.
Lead me,   Blue-beard, _____   I   will fol – low.

[5] JUDITH

El – hagy – tam   az   a – pám,   a – nyám,
I   left   my   fa – mi – ly   and   home,

39

[13] (DOOR 1)

Sostenuto (♩ = 88)

vln. (blood motif) ⌊———— 3 ————⌋ ⌊———— 3 ————⌋
clar.   xylo., picc., fl.

[14a]

Andante (assai) (♩ = 104)

2 clar.   *non legato*

⌊——— cf. no.7 ———⌋

[14b]

Molto andante Poco allegro (♩ = 108)

(vlns.)

[15a] (DOOR 2)

Allegro risoluto

2 E♭ clars., obs.

[15b] JUDITH

a tempo (♩ = 116)

p dolce   (clar.)

Itt   a   má – sik   pat – ak.
See   this   blind – ing   light here.

[16] BLUEBEARD

Sostenuto (♩ = 72)

mf

Vá – ram sö – tét tö – ve   zit – tert,
Deep with–in my cas–tle   trem – bles,

41

[17] JUDITH (DOOR 3)

Assai andante (♩ = 100)

Oh,   be   sok   kincs!
Glit – ter – ing   gold!

[18] (DOOR 4)

Lento (♩ = 80)

horn
pp

[19]

cf. no 18 - bars 1 - 4

horn / clar.

p clars.   f strings   dim.

[20] (DOOR 5)

Larghissimo (♩ = 66)

fff tutti, full organ, 4 trumpets, 4 trombones onstage

[21a] BLUEBEARD

Meno largo

ff quasi parlando, ma sempre grave

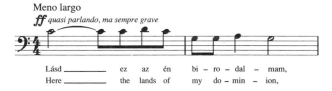

Lásd_____ ez   az   én   bi – ro – dal – mam,
Here_____ the   lands of   my   do – min – ion,

[21b] JUDITH

a tempo

p senza espessione

Szép és   nagy a   te   or – szá – god.
Yes   it   is   a   migh – ty   king – dom.

[22a]

Vivace (♩. = 80)

f

[22b]

[23]

Agitato molto (

mf

[24a] JUDITH (DOOR 6)

Tranquillo (♩ = 63)

pp sempre

Csen-des feh-ér   ta – vat   lá – tok,   Moz – du – lat – lan   feh–ér   ta – vat.
I   see   si–lent   tran-quil   wa–ters,   Mo – tion-less,   my – ste-rious   wa–ters.

[24b]

mp

[25]

Lento (♩ = 88)

(♮)

ff molto espress.

horns

[26]

Molto sostenuto (♩ = 46-48)

cf. no.23

mf

Sostenuto (♩ = 60)

strings in octaves

[28] (DOOR 7)

Molto adagio (♩ = 56)

clar.
p dolce

cor anglais

[29a] BLUEBEARD

Andante (♩ = 96)
pp

| Haj–nal–ban az | el – söt let–tem, | Pi – ros sza–gos | szép haj–nal-ban. |
| This the first I | found at dawn-ing, | In the crim-son | light of mor-ning. |

[29b]

3   *mf*   *p* dolce

[30]

Largo (♩ = 52)

f

sempre crescendo

Duke Bluebeard's Castle
A kékszakállú herceg vára

Opera in One Act, Op. 11
by Béla Bartók

Libretto by Béla Balázs

Translation by John Lloyd Davies

A kékszakállú herceg vára was first performed on May 24, 1918, at the State Opera House, Budapest. The first performance in the USA was at the City Center, New York, on October 2, 1952. The first staging in Britain was at the Rudolf Steiner Theatre, London, on January 16, 1957 by Cape Town University Opera Club. The first professional production in Britain was by Sadler's Wells Opera on October 29, 1957. This translation was made for a new production by Scottish Opera in 1989.

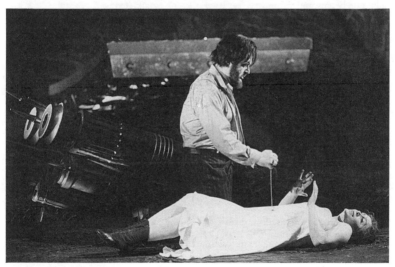

Götz Friedrich's 1985 Vienna State Opera production with Siegmund Nimsgern and Klara Takács. (photo: Österreichischer Bundestheaterverband)

CHARACTERS

The Minstrel	*speaking role*
Duke Bluebeard	*bass*
Judith	*soprano*
Three former wives	*silent*

45

The Prologue

The Minstrel appears in front of the curtain.

Once upon an ancient time . . .
A story introduced in rhyme:
The tale is old, the moral new,
Even the players could be you
Yourselves, Ladies and Gentlemen.

Haj regő rejtem
Hová, hová rejtsem
Hol volt, hol nem: kint-e vagy bent?
Régi rege, haj mit jelent,
Urak, asszonyságok?

You're watching me, I'm watching you,
But which is which and who is who?
Consider, safely in your beds
Is the theatre here, or in your heads
Ladies and Gentlemen?

Im, szólal az ének.
Ti néztek, én nézlek.
Szemünk pillás függönye fent:
Hol a színpad: kint-e vagy bent,
Urak, asszonyságok?

Here there is a generous ration:
Crimes of violence and passion —
In wars outside the blood runs redly:
Here is something far more deadly,
Ladies and Gentlemen.

Keserves és boldog
Nevezetes dolgok,
Az világ kint haddal tele,
De nem abba halunk bele,
Urak, asszonyságok.

The tale begins and we must greet it:
One by one we all repeat it.
Where it starts we cannot tell,
But we do know the ending well,
Do we not, Ladies and Gentlemen?

Nézzük egymást, nézzük,
Regénket regéljük.
Ki tudhatja honnan hozzuk?
Hallgatjuk és csodálkozzuk,
Urak, asszonyságok.

The curtain goes up behind him. The music begins.

The music starts, the play begins,
But which of us loses, and which one wins?
Is it tears or is it laughter?
Do *you* live happily ever after?
Ladies and Gentlemen?

Zene szól, a láng ég,
Kezdődjön a játék,
Szemem pillás függönye fent.
Tapsoljatok majd ha lement,
Urak, asszonyságok.

A familiar story, a familiar scene . . .
But, my friends, what does it mean?
Attend!

Régi vár, régi már
Az mese, ki róla jár,
Tik is hallgassátok.

---

* The audience is prepared for what is to follow by a prologue written in archaic folk-idiom, and spoken without music by a character impersonating a minstrel performing before an aristocratic public. The prologue begins with an untranslatable incantation formula with which epic pieces used to be introduced; it may be loosely rendered as 'Riddle my riddle'. What will follow is, then, a riddle. The next verse introduces the traditional opening line of folktales, corresponding to our 'Once upon a time'; the literal meaning of the Hungarian is, however, 'Where did it happen? Where did it not happen?' Playing upon this, the poet suggests: did it happen *inside* or *outside* (that is, inside or outside the mind)? Our old tale, the poet asks, what does it mean? There is a stage before you, but there is another inside you; your eyelids are curtains raised in front of the inner stage. What you will see, then, is a happening in the outside world, but its meaning refers to what takes place on the *inner* stage, that of the mind.

There is a reference in the prologue to wars raging in the outside world; this reference is to the First World War which was just drawing to its close when the opera had its first performance. (Both text and music had been completed before the war; the prologue was apparently written for the first performance, or the topical lines about the war were added at that time.) It is not the war 'outside' that will kill us, the poet says; death, too, is in the soul: it is spiritual death. — *Peter Bartók*

A huge, round gothic hall. On the left, a steep staircase leads to a small iron door. To the right of the staircase there are seven large doors in the wall: four of them facing the audience, two on the extreme right. Otherwise there are neither windows nor ornaments. The hall resembles an empty, dark, cold cave of stone. As the curtains part, the stage is in complete darkness, in which the minstrel disappears. [1, 2]

Suddenly the small iron door opens and in a dazzling white square beam of light emanating from it the silhouettes of Bluebeard and Judith appear.

BLUEBEARD

We have arrived.	Megérkeztünk.
Here you stand alone with Bluebeard	[3] Íme lássad: ez a Kékszakállú vára.
and his castle,	
So unlike your joyful homeland.	Nem tündököl, mint atyádé.
Judith tell me, will you follow?	Judit, jössz-e még utánam?

JUDITH

Lead me Bluebeard, I will follow.	[4] Megyek, megyek, Kékszakállú.

BLUEBEARD

He comes down a few steps.

Hear the bells of sorrow ringing?	Nem hallod a vészharangot?
For the love your mother gave you.	Anyád gyászba öltözködött,
See your father bringing weapons,	Atyád éles kardot szijjaz,
See your brother ride to save you.	Testvérbátyád lovat nyergel.
Judith, tell me, will you follow?	Judit, jössz-e még utánam?

JUDITH

Lead me Bluebeard, I will follow.	Megyek, megyek, Kékszakállú.

Bluebeard comes all the way down the steps and turns towards Judith, who has stopped midway. The beam of light shining through the door illuminates them and the stairway.

BLUEBEARD

Hesitating? Are you frightened?	Megállsz Judit? Mennél vissza?

JUDITH

her hands pressed against her breast

No . . . my skirt was caught on	Nem. A szoknyám akadt csak fel,
something,	
Something touched me in the darkness.	Felakadt szép selyemszoknyám.

BLUEBEARD

See the doorway still lies open.	Nyitva van még fent az ajtó.

JUDITH

No, my Bluebeard!	Kékszakállú!

She comes down a few steps.

I left my family and home,	[5] Elhagytam az apám, anyám,
I left my brother all alone,	Elhagytam szép testvérbátyám,

She comes down all the way.

I left my intended bridegroom,	Elhagytam a vőlegényem,
To follow you, to be with you.	Hogy váradba eljöhessek.

She pushes herself close against Bluebeard.

O my Bluebeard! If you leave me,	Kékszakállú! Ha kiűznél,
If you should abandon me now,	Küszöbödnél megállanék,
I'll stay here upon your threshold.	Küszöbödre lefeküdnék.

Bluebeard takes her in his arms.

BLUEBEARD

Let the door be shut behind you.	Most csukódjon be az ajtó.

47

The small iron door closes above them. The hall remains only light enough for the two human shapes and the seven large black doors to be visible.

JUDITH

Holding on to Bluebeard's hand, she feels her way along the left wall.

Finally in Bluebeard's castle!	[6] Ez a Kékszakállú vára!
But no windows? But no daylight?	Nincsen ablak? Nincsen erkély?

BLUEBEARD

Nothing.	Nincsen.

JUDITH

No light from the sun reaches here?	Hiába is süt kint a nap?

BLUEBEARD

Nothing.	Hiába.

JUDITH

Cold for ever? Dark for ever?	Hideg marad? Sötét marad?

BLUEBEARD

Coldness . . . darkness . . .	Hideg . . . sötét . . .

JUDITH

She comes forward.

In this darkness every whisper	Ki ezt látná, jaj, nem szólna,
Will be silent, every rumour . . .	Suttogó hír elhalkulna.

BLUEBEARD

What have you heard?	Hírt hallottál?

JUDITH

All your castle lies in darkness!	Milyen sötét a te várad!

She feels her way on. She shudders.

It is wet here my beloved.	[7] Vizes a fal! Kékszakállú!
What's this liquid in your castle?	Milyen víz hull a kezemre?
Is it weeping? Is it weeping?	Sir a várad! Sir a várad!

She covers her eyes.

BLUEBEARD

Judith, Judith, would you not be	Ugy-e, Judit, jobb volna most
Happy now with your intended:	Vőlegényed kastélyában:
Where the white walls meet the sunlight,	Fehér falon fut a rózsa,
Where the roses greet the sunlight?	Cseréptetőn táncol a nap.

JUDITH

Never, never. O my Bluebeard!	[8] Ne bánts, ne bánts Kékszakállú!
What are roses, what is sunlight?	Nem kell rózsa, nem kell napfény!
What are roses, what is sunlight?	Nem kell rózsa, nem kell napfény!
Nothing . . . nothing . . . nothing . . .	Nem kell . . . Nem kell . . . Nem kell . . .
In your castle all is darkness,	Milyen sötét a te várad!
In your castle all is darkness,	Milyen sötét a te várad!
All is darkness . . .	Milyen sötét . . .
And cold, and cold! O my Bluebeard!	Szegény, szegény Kékszakállú!

Crying, she falls on her knees before Bluebeard and kisses his hands.

BLUEBEARD

Tell me why you came here, Judith.	Miért jöttél hozzám, Judit?

48

I shall warm the cold and darkness,	Nedves falát felszárítom,
With my body burn up the tears.	Ajakammal szárítom fel!
Till the frozen stone is glowing,	Hideg kövét melegítem,
With my passion set it glowing,	A testemmel melegítem.
With my own flesh, with my own blood,	Ugy-e szabad, ugy-e szabad,
O my Bluebeard!	Kékszakállú!
Love will conquer all your sadness,	Nem lesz sötét a te várad,
I will open up the darkness.	Negnyitjuk a falat ketten.
Light will shine here, breezes blow here,	Szél bejárjon, nap besüssön, nap besüssön,
love will live here,	
In this house as light unending.	Tündököljön a te várad!

BLUEBEARD

Nothing here can pierce the darkness.	Nem tündököl az én váram.

JUDITH
She walks further in, to the right.

Lead me further, my beloved,	Gyere vezess, Kékszakállú,
Lead me further in your castle.	Mindenhova vezess engem.

She walks on further.

Ah, what are those seven doorways,	Nagy csukott ajtókat látok,
Seven black and bolted doorways?	Hét fekete csukott ajtót!

Bluebeard follows her with his eyes without moving or talking.

Tell me what they mean my Bluebeard.	Mért vannak az ajtók csukva?

BLUEBEARD

So that none may learn my secrets.	Hogy ne lásson bele senki.

JUDITH
[9]

Open, open, let them open!	Nyisd ki, nyisd ki! Nekem nyisd ki!
All the doors must now be open!	Minden ajtó legyen nyitva!
Let the light in, let the air in!	Szél bejárjon, nap besüssön!

BLUEBEARD

But remember all the rumours.	Emlékezz rá, milyen hír jár.

JUDITH

Let the castle greet the daylight,	A te várad derüljön fel,
Let the castle greet the daylight!	A te várad derüljön fel,
Bitter, bitter, joyless castle,	Szegény, sötét, hideg várad!
Open! Open! Open! [8]	Nyisd ki! Nyisd ki! Nyisd ki!

She hammers on the first door. As though in reply, a cavernous sigh is heard, like night winds sighing down long, dismal corridors. [10] She steps back to Bluebeard.

Ah! Ah! What was that? What was sighing? [1]	Jaj! Jaj! Mi volt ez? Mi sóhajtott?
Who was sighing? Tell me Bluebeard!	Ki sóhajtott? Kékszakállú!
It's your castle! It's your castle! It's your castle!	A te várad! A te várad! A te várad!

BLUEBEARD

Frightened?	Félsz-e?

JUDITH
gently, weeping

Oh, I heard your castle sighing!	Oh, a várad felsóhajtott!

BLUEBEARD

Frightened?	Félsz?

49

Oh, I heard your castle sighing!	Oh, a várad felsóhajtott!
Let's unlock it, both together.	Gyere nyissuk, velem gyere.
I will unlock it, I alone.	[12] Én akarom kinyitni, én!
Softly and gently I will do it.	Szépen, halkan fogom nyitni,
Softly, gently, gently.	Halkan, puhán, halkan.
O my love, give me the keys now,	Kékszakállú, add a kulcsot,
Give me the keys, for I love you.	Add a kulcsot, mert szeretlek!

She leans on Bluebeard's shoulder.

BLUEBEARD

Heaven bless your sweet hands, Judith.	Áldott a te kezed, Judit.

The bundle of keys rattles in the dark.

JUDITH

Thank you, thank you.	Köszönöm, köszönöm!

She walks back to the first door.

I alone will open the door!	Én akarom kinyitni, én!

As the lock turns, the underground sigh is heard again.

Listen, listen.	Hallod? Hallod?

The door opens up, leaving, like a wound, a blood-red square opening in the wall. From deep within, the bloody glow casts a long beam of light on the floor of the hall. [13]

BLUEBEARD

What's there? What's there?	Mit látsz? Mit látsz?

JUDITH
her hands against her breast

Shackles, knife-blades, torture tables,	Láncok, kések, szöges karók,
Red hot irons . . .	Izzó nyársak . . .

BLUEBEARD

It's my torture chamber, Judith.	Ez a kínzókamra, Judit.

JUDITH

Cruel is your torture chamber,	Szörnyű a te kínzókamrád,
O my Bluebeard! Cruel! Cruel!	Kékszakállú! Szörnyű! Szörnyű!

BLUEBEARD

Frightened?	Félsz-e?

JUDITH
She shudders. [7, 14a]

All your castle walls are bleeding,	A te várad fala véres!
Yes, your castle's bleeding, bleeding!	A te várad vérzik! Véres . . . Vérzik . . .

BLUEBEARD

Frightened?	Félsz-e?

JUDITH
She turns around towards Bluebeard. Her silhouette glows in the red light. She speaks with pale, quiet determination.

No, not frightened.	Nem! Nem félek.
The daylight comes. Dawn is breaking.	Nézd, derül mar. Ugy-e derül?

She returns to Bluebeard, carefully along the edge of the beam of light.

The daylight comes! See this dazzling brilliance.	Nézd ezt a fényt. Látod? Szép fénypatak.

She kneels and holds her open palms to the light.

50

Tainted brilliance, blood-stained beauty.	Piros patak, véres patak.

JUDITH
She stands up.

Look now, look now, dawning daybreak, [14b]	Nézd csak, nézd csak, hogy dereng már!
See the sunlight!	Nézd csak, nézd csak!
Every door must now be opened,	Minden ajtót ki kell nyitni!
Giving us fresh air and sunlight,	Szél bejárjon, nap besüssön,
Every door must now be opened.	Minden ajtót ki kell nyitni!

BLUEBEARD

You don't know what lies behind them.	Nem tudod, mi van mögöttük.

JUDITH

Give me keys to every doorway!	Add ide a többi kulcsot!
Give me keys to every doorway!	Add ide a többi kulcsot!
I will open every doorway.	Minden ajtót ki kell nyitni!
Open quickly!	Minden ajtót!

BLUEBEARD

Judith, tell me why you want to.	Judit, Judit, mért akarod?

JUDITH

I love you.	Mert szeretlek!

BLUEBEARD

Deep within, my castle trembles,	Váram sötét töve reszket,
You may open them or close them.	Nyithatsz, csukhatsz minden ajtót.

He gives Judith the second key. Their hands meet in the light.

Take care, take care in my castle,	Vigyázz, vigyázz a váramra,
For us both be careful, Judith.	Vigyázz, vigyázz miránk, Judit!

JUDITH
She goes to the second door.

Softly, gently I will do it,	Szépen, halkan fogom nyitni,
Softly, gently.	Szépen, halkan.

The lock turns and the second door opens up. Its opening is yellow-red, but also dark and frightening. The second lightbeam falls on the floor next to the first one. [15a]

BLUEBEARD

What's there?	Mit látsz?

JUDITH

Thousands of appalling weapons,	Száz kegyetlen szörnyű fegyver,
Instruments of terrible war.	Sok rettentő hadi szerszám.

BLUEBEARD

Now my armoury is open.	Ez a fegyveresház, Judit.

JUDITH

You are strong and full of power,	Milyen nagyon erős vagy te,
Oh, but hard your pitiless heart!	Milyen nagy kegyetlen vagy te!

BLUEBEARD

Frightened?	Félsz-e?

JUDITH
[7]

Blood has stained your cruel weapons,	Vér szárad a fegyvereken,
Blood anointed all your weapons.	Véres a sok hadiszerszám!

She turns back towards Bluebeard.

BLUEBEARD

Frightened?   Félsz-e?

JUDITH

Give me keys to all the other doorways!   Add ide a többi kulcsot!

BLUEBEARD

Judith, Judith!   Judit, Judit!

JUDITH

She returns slowly along the second light beam.

See this blinding light here,   [15b] Itt a másik patak,
Can't you see it? See it, see it!   Szép fénypatak. Látod? Látod?
Give me the keys to all the doorways.   Add ide a többi kulcsot!

BLUEBEARD

For both of us be careful, Judith.   Vigyázz, vigyázz miránk, Judit!

JUDITH

Give me the keys to all the doorways!   Add ide a többi kulcsot!

BLUEBEARD

You don't know what lies behind them.   Nem tudod, mit rejt az ajtó.

JUDITH

I have come here, for I love you.   Ide jöttem, mert szeretlek.
I am here and only for you.   Itt vagyok, a tied vagyok.
Let me see your castle Bluebeard,   Most már vezess mindenhová,
Let each door be open for me.   Most már nyiss ki minden ajtót!

BLUEBEARD

Deep within, my castle trembles,   [16] Váram sötét töve reszket,
Stones cry out in exultation.   Bús sziklából gyönyör borzong.
Judith, Judith! Cool and fresh from   Judit, Judit! Hűs és édes,
Open wounds the blood runs freely.   Nyitott sebből vér ha ömlik.

JUDITH

I came here because I love you: Ide jöttem, mert szeretlek,
Let each door be open for me.   Most már nyiss ki minden ajtót.

BLUEBEARD

Here are keys to three more doorways.   Adok neked három kulcsot.
You may look but ask no questions,   Látni forgsz, de sohse kérdezz.
Look but not a single question.   Akármit látsz, sohse kérdezz!

He hands them to her.

JUDITH

Give me now the keys you promised.   Add ide a három kulcsot!

She takes them impatiently, rushes to the third door, but stops in front of it, hesitating.

BLUEBEARD

But why stop now? Get it open!   Mért álltál meg? Mért nem nyitod?

JUDITH

But I cannot find the key-hole.   Kezem a zárt nem találja.

BLUEBEARD

Don't be frightened, nothing matters.   Judit, ne félj, most már mindegy.

She turns the key. The door opens with a deep, warm, metallic sound. A golden beam of light shines next to the other two on the floor.

52

Above: Andrés Békés, 1989 Hungarian State Opera production with Ildikó Komlosi and Kolos Kováts. (photo: MTI, Budapest).
Below: ENO's 1981 revival with Elizabeth Connell and John Tomlinson directed by Glen Byam Shaw and designed by Ralph Koltai.

JUDITH

Glittering gold, glittering gold!	[17] Oh, be sok kincs! Oh, be sok kincs!

She kneels and digs into the treasure, placing jewels, a crown and a mantle on the doorstep.

Golden coins and diamonds	Aranypénz és drága gyémánt,
And emeralds and precious rubies,	Bélagyönggyel fényes ékszer,
Jewelled crowns and fine apparel.	Koronák és dús palástok!

BLUEBEARD

It's my castle's treasure chamber.	Ez a váram kincsesháza.

JUDITH

You are rich indeed my Bluebeard.	Mily gazdag vagy Kékszakállú!

BLUEBEARD

All of this is yours forever,	Tied most már mind ez a kincs,
All the jewels and all the treasure.	Tied arany, gyöngy és gyémánt.

JUDITH
[7] *She suddenly stands up.*

There is blood on all your treasure!	Vérfolt van az ékszereken!
And the crown's covered in bloodstains!	Legszebbik koronád véres!

Puzzled, she turns towards Bluebeard.

BLUEBEARD

The fourth door is waiting for you.	Nyisd ki a negyedik ajtót.
Bring the light in — open, open!	Legyen napfény, nyissad, nyissad . . .

She becomes more restless and impatient. She turns to the fourth door and quickly opens it. From the doorway flowery branches push inward, and the opening in the wall is a square of blue-green. The new lightbeam shines next to the others on the floor. [18, 19]

JUDITH

Oh! Lovely flowers, Oh! Beautiful scents! [19]	Oh! virágok! Oh! illatos kert!
Hidden in the stony darkness.	Kemény sziklák alatt rejtve.

BLUEBEARD

It's my castle's secret garden.	Ez a váram rejtett kertje.

JUDITH

Oh! Lovely flowers!	Oh! virágok!
Slender lilies tall as men,	Embernyi nagy liljomok,
Snowy white, beautiful roses,	Hűs-fehér patyolat rózsák,
Red carnations, glowing with light!	Piros szekfűk szórják a fényt.
Unimaginable beauty!	Sohse láttam ilyen kertet.

BLUEBEARD

Here the flowers kneel before you,	Minden virág neked bókol,
Here the flowers kneel before you.	Minden virág neked bókol.
You will tend them, you will tend them,	Te fakasztod, te hervasztod,
And new life your love will send them.	Szebben újra te sarjasztod.

JUDITH
[7] *She suddenly bends down.*

Every single rose is blood-stained,	Fehér rózsád töve véres,
Every blade of grass is blood-stained!	Virágaid földje véres!

BLUEBEARD

Opening their petals for you,	Szemed nyitja kelyheiket,
At dawn waking, blooming for you.	S neked csengetyűznek reggel.

JUDITH
She stands up and turns towards Bluebeard.

54

Who has given blood to feed them?	Ki öntözte kerted földjét?

BLUEBEARD

Judith, love me, do not ask me.	Judit szeress, sohse kérdezz.
Look the daylight is returning.	Nézd, hogy derül már a váram.
Quickly now unlock the fifth door.	Nyisd ki az ötödik ajtót!

With a quick movement Judith runs to the fifth door and flings it open. A high balcony and a far landscape are seen; light pours in in a brilliant flood. [20]

JUDITH

Ah!	Ah!

Blinded, she holds up her hands to shield her eyes.

BLUEBEARD

Here the lands of my dominion,	[21a] Lásd, ez az én birodalmam,
In this realm I am the master.	Messze néző szép könyöklőm.
Is it not a mighty kingdom?	Ugye hogy szép nagy, nagy ország?

JUDITH

She is looking out stiffly and absent-mindedly.

Yes it is a mighty kingdom.	[21b] Szép és nagy a te országod.

BLUEBEARD

Velvet forests, silky meadows,	Selyemrétek, bársonyerdők,
Silver sounds of rivers running,	Hosszú ezüst folyók folynak,
Far away majestic mountains.	És kék hegyek nagyon messze.

JUDITH

Yes it is a mighty kingdom.	Szép és nagy a te országod.

BLUEBEARD

All of this is yours, my Judith.	Most már Judit mind a tied,
Dawn and twilight, noontime and night.	Itt lakik a hajnal, alkony,
Sun and moon and stars belong here,	Itt lakik nap, hold és csillag,
They will play with you for ever.	S leszen neked játszótársad.

JUDITH

But the clouds cast bloody shadows!	Véres árnyat vet a felhő!
What's the meaning of these storm clouds?	Milyen felhők szállnak ottan?

BLUEBEARD

Look, look at my castle shining,	[22a] Nézd, tündököl az én váram,
You deliver me from darkness.	Áldott kezed ezt művelte,
Your fair hand has done this, Judith.	Áldott a te kezed, áldott.

He opens his arms.

Come now, come now, let me hold you.	[22b] Gyere, gyere, tedd szivemre.

She does not move.

JUDITH

But two doors remain unopened.	De két ajtó csukva van még.

BLUEBEARD

Never will those doorways open.	Legyen csukva a két ajtó.
Let the castle ring with music.	Teljen dallal az én váram.
Come now, come, I long to kiss you!	Gyere, gyere, csókra várlak!

JUDITH

Let the final doors be opened!	Nyissad ki még a két ajtót!

55

Judith, Judith, love me, love me,	Judit, Judit, csókra várlak.
Hold me, love me, Judith, love me!	Gyere, várlak. Judit, várlak!

JUDITH

Let the final doors be opened!	Nyissad ki még a két ajtót!

BLUEBEARD

Did you not want to bring light here,	Azt akartad, felderüljön;
See — glittering the castle walls.	Nézd, tündököl már a váram.

JUDITH
[23]

I won't have a single door here	Nem akarom, hogy előttem
Shut against me. If you love me ...	Csukott ajtóid legyenek!

BLUEBEARD

Careful, careful, in my castle,	Vigyázz, vigyázz a váramra,
Or the light will turn to darkness.	Vigyázz, nem lesz fényesebb már.

JUDITH

I will fear no danger from you my	Életemet, halálomat, Kékszakállú,
beloved.	
Open every single doorway, Bluebeard,	Nyissad ki még a két ajtót, Kékszakállú!
Bluebeard!	Kékszakállú!

BLUEBEARD

Let it be now, let it be now,	Mért akarod, mért akarod?
Judith! Judith!	Judit! Judit!

JUDITH

Open, open.	Nyissad, nyissad!

BLUEBEARD

Come and take it then. One more key.	Adok neked még egy kulcsot.

Judith, silent, holds out a demanding hand. Bluebeard hands her the key. She goes to the sixth door. As the key turns in the lock, a deep crying sound is heard. Judith steps back.

Judith, Judith, leave it alone!	Judit, Judit, ne nyissad ki!

Judith quickly steps to the door and opens it. As if a shadow was cast over it, the hall becomes slightly darker.

JUDITH

I see silent tranquil waters,	[24a] Csendes fehér tavat látok,
Motionless mysterious waters.	Mozdulatlan fehér tavat.
[24b]	
Tell me what it means, beloved.	Milyen víz ez Kékszakállú?

BLUEBEARD

Weeping, Judith, weeping, weeping.	Könnyek, Judit, könnyek, könnyek.

JUDITH

Silent and mysterious waters.	Milyen néma, mozdulatlan.

BLUEBEARD

Weeping, Judith, weeping, weeping.	Könnyek, Judit, könnyek, könnyek.

JUDITH
She bends down and examines the lake.

Mysterious transparency.	Sima fehér, tiszta fehér.

BLUEBEARD

Weeping, Judith, weeping, weeping.	Könnyek, Judit, könnyek, könnyek.

Judith slowly turns round, and without a word looks into Bluebeard's eyes.

BLUEBEARD
He opens his arms.

Come my Judith, come my Judith, let
me kiss you.

Gyere Judit, gyere Judit, csókra várlak.

Judith does not move.

Come I'm waiting Judith, waiting.

Gyere várlak, Judit, várlak.

She still does not move.

The final door never opens,
Never opens.

Az utolsót nem nyitom ki.
Nem nyitom ki.

With her head cast down, she slowly goes to Bluebeard. As if begging almost sadly, she leans towards him.

JUDITH

O my Bluebeard, take me, love me.

Kékszakállú . . . szeress engem.

Bluebeard embraces her. A long kiss. [25] *Then, with her head on Bluebeard's shoulder:*
Do you love me truly Bluebeard?   Nagyon szeretsz, Kékszakállú?

BLUEBEARD

You have brought me light from
darkness,
Kiss me, kiss me, ask me nothing.

Te vagy váram fényessége,

Csókolj, csókolj, sohse kérdezz.

A long kiss.

JUDITH
her head on Bluebeard's shoulder

Tell me truly me beloved,
Who possessed your love before me?

Mondd meg nekem Kékszakállú,
Kit szerettél én előttem?

BLUEBEARD

You bring sunlight into darkness,
Kiss me, kiss me, ask me nothing.

Te vagy váram fényessége,
Csókolj, csókolj, sohse kérdezz.

JUDITH

Tell me of the way you loved them,
Fairer than me? Dearer than me?
More than you love me, beloved?

[26] Mondd meg nekem, hogy szeretted?
Szebb volt mint én? Más volt mint én?
Mondd el nekem, Kékszakállú.

BLUEBEARD

Judith love me, ask me nothing.

Judit szeress, sohse kérdezz.

JUDITH

Answer me the truth, beloved.

Mondd el nekem, Kékszakállú.

BLUEBEARD

Judith love me, ask me nothing.

Judit szeress, sohse kérdezz.

JUDITH
separating herself from the embrace

Open the seventh door now!

Nyisd ki a hetedik ajtót!

Bluebeard does not answer.

I know what's behind it, Bluebeard,
What the seventh door is hiding!
Blood upon your walls and weapons,
Blood upon your precious jewels,
Bloodstained flowers in your garden,
Bloodstained clouds across your heavens!
Now I understand it, Bluebeard.
I know where the weeping came from:
All your other women lie there,

Tudom, tudom, Kékszakállú,
Mit rejt a hetedik ajtó.
Vér szárad a fegyvereken,
Legszebbik koronád véres,
Virágaid földje véres,
Véres árnyat vet a felhő!
Tudom, tudom, Kékszakállú,
Fehér könnytó kinek könnye.
Ott van mind a régi asszony

57

Brutally destroyed and murdered. True the rumours, true about you.	Legyilkolva, vérbefagyva. Jaj, igaz hír, suttogó hír.

BLUEBEARD

Judith!	Judit!

JUDITH

It's true! It's true! I must know the terrible truth. Open the seventh door now!	Igaz, igaz! Most én tudni akarom már. Nyisd ki a hetedik ajtót!

[26]

BLUEBEARD

Take it . . . take it . . . Here's the seventh key.	Fogjad . . . fogjad . . . Itt a hetedik kulcs.

Judith looks at it stiffly, and does not reach for it. [27]

When the door is open Judith, You will see my wives are waiting.	Nyisd ki, Judit, lássad őket, Ott van mind a régi asszony.

Judith remains motionless for some time. Then she takes the key with slow, uncertain hands, and goes to the door slowly, unsteadily, and opens it. As the key turns in the lock, the sixth and fifth doors close with a soft sigh. It becomes much darker. The hall is lit only by the coloured light streaming from the four doorways opposite. And then the seventh door opens and silver moonlight streams through it illuminating Judith's and Bluebeard's faces. [28]

BLUEBEARD

See, the ones I loved before you, All have known my love before you.	Lásd a régi asszonyokat, Lásd, akiket én szerettem.

JUDITH
steps back, amazed

Living, living, they're still living!	Élnek, élnek, itten élnek!

The former wives come from the seventh doorway. They are three, have crowns and are loaded with glorious jewels. They proceed, pale-faced, one after the other, with proud bearing, and they stop in front of Bluebeard, who kneels down in front of them.

BLUEBEARD
with his arms open, as if dreaming

Beauty, beauty, perfect beauty. They will always live beside me. They have brought me all my treasure, With their blood they feed the flowers, They have built this mighty kingdom, Judith, theirs is all my castle.	Szépek, szépek, százszor szépek. Mindig voltak, mindig éltek. Sok kincsemet ők gyüjtötték, Virágaim ők öntözték, Birodalmam növesztették, Övék minden, minden, minden.

JUDITH
She stands next to the former wives as the fourth one, her shoulders bent and tense.

With their beauty, with their riches, I am nothing, nothing at all.	Milyen szépek, milyen dúsak, Én, jaj, koldus, kopott vagyok.

BLUEBEARD
He stands up. With a soft voice:

This the first I found at dawning, In the crimson light of morning. She possesses every sunrise, Hers the glowing gown of daybreak, Hers the shining crown of silver, And hers each new day forever.	[29a] Hajnalban az elsőt leltem, Piros szagos szép hajnalban. Övé most már minden hajnal, Övé piros hűs palástja, Övé ezüst koronája, Övé most már minden hajnal.

JUDITH

Next to her I'm less than nothing.	Jaj, szebb nálam, dúsabb nálam!

58

BLUEBEARD

In the day I found the second,	Másodikat délben leltem,
Golden, blazing in the hot noon.	Néma, égő, arany délben.
She possesses every midday,	Minden dél az övé most már.
Hers the flaming fire mantle,	Övé nehéz tűzpalástja,
Hers the crown of burning sunlight,	Övé arany koronája,
Hers the heat of day forever.	Minden dél az övé most már.

JUDITH

Next to her I'm less than nothing.	Jaj, szebb nálam, dúsabb nálam!

The second wife returns.

BLUEBEARD

Eventide revealed the third one,	Harmadikat este leltem,
In the slow and sombre twilight.	Békés bágyadt barna este.
Her time is the time of sunset,	Övé most már minden este,
Hers to wear the darkened mantle,	Övé barna búpalástja,
As the sun is disappearing.	Övé most már minden este.

JUDITH

Next to her I'm less than nothing.	Jaj! szebb nálam, dúsabb nálam!

The third wife returns. Bluebeard stops in front of Judith. For a long time they look into each other's eyes. The fourth door slowly closes.

BLUEBEARD

Then I found the fourth at midnight.	Negyediket éjjel leltem,

JUDITH

Bluebeard, Bluebeard! No more, no more!	Kékszakállú, megállj, megállj!

BLUEBEARD

In the starry gown of midnight . . .	Csillagos fekete éjjel.

JUDITH

No more, no more! I am still here!	Hallgass, hallgass, itt vagyok még!

BLUEBEARD

And your face possessed by starlight,	Fehér arcod sütött fénnyel,
Dancing in the beauty of your hair,	Barna hajad felhőt hajtott,
Every night is yours forever.	Tied lesz már minden éjjel.

He goes to the third door and fetches the crown, mantle and jewels which Judith previously put on the doorstep. The third door closes. He places the mantle on Judith's shoulders.

JUDITH

My beloved, spare me, spare me!	Kékszakállú nem kell, nem kell!

BLUEBEARD

Ever more the starry mantle . . .	Tied csillagos palástja . . .

He places the crown on Judith's head.

JUDITH

Spare me, Bluebeard, take it off me!	Jaj, jaj, Kékszakállú vedd le!

BLUEBEARD

Ever more the jewels upon you,	Tied gyémánt koronája,

He puts the jewels around Judith's neck.

Ever the best of my treasures,	Tied a legdrágább kincsem,
Beauty, beauty, never changing,	Szép vagy, szép vagy, százszor szép vagy,
Ever queen of all my beauties,	Te voltál a legszebb asszony,
Ever beautiful!	A legszebb asszony!

They look at each other for a long time. Judith stoops under the weight of the mantle, her head bent beneath the diamond crown, and she follows the other wives along the silvery beam of light through the seventh door. [30] *It shuts.*

Now all shall be darkness ...

Darkness ... darkness ...

És mindég is éjjel lesz már ...

Éjjel ... éjjel ...

Complete darkness, and Bluebeard disappears in it.

Monte Jaffe and Kathryn Harries in Scottish Opera's production designed and directed by Stefanos Lazaridis, 1989. (photo: Peter Devlin)

'The Wooden Prince': A Tale for Adults

Ferenc Bónis

Reviewing the First Night of *Duke Bluebeard's Castle* in 1918, Zoltán Kodály was the first to point out that Bartók's stage works form a tightly-woven unit. 'The strength of the way the music is constructed is even more evident if we listen to *The Wooden Prince* after *Duke Bluebeard's Castle*. The ballet balances the opera's despairing *adagio* with a playful, vivid *allegro*. The two works come together like movements in a gigantic symphony. And anyone who thinks of atonality as Bartók's main achievement should note that both pieces have a recurring fundamental modality, just as in Mozart's operas.' To the 'two movements of a gigantic symphony' we may now add a finale of sweeping strength, the pantomime of *The Miraculous Mandarin*.

The differences between Bartók's stage works are obvious but what is the thread which binds them together? All three explore the mysteries of the relationship between men and women. In Wagnerian terms, they pose the question whether Man, suffering and alone, can be saved by the selfless and self-sacrificing love of Woman. Each piece offers a different answer. As Kodály wrote, the opera 'demonstrates the eternally unresolved argument of Man and Woman'; the pantomime demonstrates the catharsis of love in death, or the triumph of passion over death; and although *The Wooden Prince* has the traditional happy ending of a folktale, it is a parable which casts serious doubt as to the consequences.

The libretto of *The Wooden Prince* appeared in the Budapest literary magazine *Nyugat* (West) at Christmas 1912, a year after the completion of *Bluebeard*. Musicologists previously thought that *The Miraculous Mandarin* was conceived after the Ballets Russes tour that year to Budapest, but it is much more likely that Diaghilev's company inspired the creation of *The Wooden Prince*. It is also probable that the author, Béla Balázs, had already given the story in manuscript to Bartók. In 1918 Balázs wrote: 'My ballet-story was written especially to please Bartók.' Balázs sometimes remembers things incorrectly in his memoirs but Bartók himself authenticated this remark in an interview before the first performance of the ballet: 'the indifference towards my one-act opera *Duke Bluebeard's Castle* gave me the impulse to compose this ballet. As is well known, my opera failed when I entered it for a competition. [. . .] But I love it very much. So much so, that when I received the libretto from Béla Balázs, I immediately imagined a spectacular, rich, colourful ballet which, with its dynamic story-line, would make it possible for the two to be staged at one performance.'

The first date on the preliminary sketches of *The Wooden Prince* is April 1914, and in 1918 Bartók remembered: 'I started composing my ballet before war broke out, and then I ceased work on it for a long time. My life was in a turmoil. Then, last season, István Strasser gave the first performances of my symphonic piece *Two Portraits*, the second part of which (*The Freak*) I heard performed by an orchestra for the first time. This inspired me to complete *The Wooden Prince* and soon I had done so.' Strasser's concert was on April 20, 1916. Immediately afterwards Bartók set off on a folksong collecting tour in the country, returning during the first half of May. He could only have completed the ballet after his return. On July 14 he wrote to Count Miklós Bánffy, Intendant of the Budapest Opera House, that the 'piano score of the

The Hungarian State Ballet's production of 'The Wooden Prince' choreographed by László Seregi, 1981. (photo: Wlodzimierz Malek)

ballet is now ready and it has been copied. I could play it for you on 21st, 22nd, or 24th.' On November 7, Bartók submitted the piano score and one third of the orchestral score. He finished the orchestration towards the end of January 1917 and on February 5 he handed in the full score. In letters to his family outside Budapest, Bartók reported on the dance rehearsals on February 22, and the first orchestral rehearsal on April 18. The première, conducted by Egisto Tango, was a triumph for the composer, after many years of neglect.

The process leading towards this performance had not been smooth. Despite the 'poetic' details of Balázs' memoirs (written in 1947), they contain a reasonably authentic account of the atmosphere before the première:

At the time seven conductors were employed at the Opera. All seven refused to conduct 'such messy music'. In the end the eminent Italian guest conductor Egisto Tango took it up. The Opera House had two producers but neither wished to be involved, intent as they were on protecting the honour of their theatre from 'this assault against art'. There was a *maître de ballet* — a kind of kinesthetics teacher, rather meek. He was appalled by the score: no waltz, no polka, no minuet, no czardàs — what could he teach the *corps de ballet*? So he resigned as well. The Hungarian Royal Opera House went on strike. They were all in revolt. I cannot remember any wage dispute or political issue in which the Opera staff had ever taken such a staunch position as they did when they turned against Bartók's music. He did not involve himself in the affair, and I was careful not to tell him anything. I was no more than a modest young librarian in the Municipal Library of Education. But I knew that this was a matter of life and death as far as he was concerned, so I went to the Intendant's office and told Count Bánffy: 'Sir, I have never been on stage in my life. Let me produce this ballet. I have no idea how to teach movements and steps, but let me have a go — or else you will have to cancel the première.'

Such an offer would surely have been turned down by any other other opera director in the world, and it took a Hungarian count to take the risk. But Count Miklós Bánffy was a very gifted aristocrat — a fine painter and a writer. Apart from directing the Opera, he was a land-owner and, for a while, Hungary's Minister for Foreign Affairs. Kodály wanted to use one of his plays as an opera libretto but failed to get the author's permission. Bánffy had himself designed the sets and costumes for *The Wooden Prince*, and, in order to save the performances, he accepted Balázs' unusual offer. The poster for the première duly lists Balázs as producer. As for the choreography, Balázs' memoirs should be treated with caution. A contemporary magazine (*Magyar Szinpad/Hungarian Stage*) reported: 'The librettist had occasion when he staged the ballet to enrich the choreography of the ballet master (Ottó Zöbisch) with a number of ideas and colours.' Balázs remembered the première: 'The ticket prices were raised steeply. They were preparing for a huge opera scandal. Reviews were written beforehand to the effect 'Why do you keep on composing, Béla?' And it was a memorable evening. After the last note of the music had died away, there was total silence. No clapping. No hisses and catcalls either. An enormous balance seemed to swing in the air. The audience fought with their feelings in silence. Then the sound of ecstatic applause and bravos exploded from the gallery and cascaded, like an avalanche, down to the boxes and the stalls, carrying even the rabble of the press with it. Many reviews had to be rewritten that night. It was Bartók's first great success.'

Bartók himself regarded it as an important day in his life, and recorded it, in his matter-of-fact manner, in his autobiography. '1917 marked a decisive change in the attitude of the Budapest public towards my music. I experienced a performance of my ballet *The Wooden Prince*, which was musically perfect under Egisto Tango's baton.'

*

The libretto is about two young people finding each other, and their struggle to fulfil their love. As in *The Magic Flute*, they must overcome both the tests which the world sets up and their own weaknesses: vanity, indifference, and the appeal of the superficially brilliant. The folktale also introduces other themes. Nature plays an important role, both hostile and protective; a few years later it would become clear that Nature was Bartók's true spiritual home. Another theme is the relationship of the sexes, an issue with resonances of Wagner and Ibsen. Balázs decribed the ballet as 'the tragedy of the artist'. He continued: 'The wooden puppet made by my Prince to be his messenger announcing his presence to the Princess is the image representing the artist's work. All he possesses is put into the image, which shines in its perfection, while the artist remains without anything. I was referring here to that all-too-frequent case when a work of art becomes the rival of its own creator, and to that painful moment when a woman prefers a poem to the poet, a painting to the painter.'

The idea of an animated puppet and of a fairy who brings it to life resembles Stravinsky's *Petrushka*, where the Magician makes his puppets dance and tragedy ensues when the Ballerina falls in love with the handsome Moor instead of the warm-hearted Petrushka. Bartók only hints at this and opts instead for a happy ending in which the hero is adored by Nature. Yet there is an undertone of tragedy in the folktale.

Before the first performance Bartók spoke of the symphonic conception of the score:

> The music of this ballet has been conceived as a kind of symphonic poem for dance. It has three clearly defined parts and each part is divided into sections. The first part ends with the dance of the Wooden Prince and the Princess. The second, which ends with the reappearance of the Wooden Prince, is more serene, and acts as a middle movement. The third part is a repeat of the first but with its sections in reverse order, as the libretto demands.

This division into three parts is a simplification; the score really has five parts, in a 'bridge' construction. The form recurs in many of his most important works, from the Fourth String Quartet, to the Second Piano Concerto and the Fifth String Quartet. In the ballet it develops like this:

The awakening of Nature.

The Prince falls in love with the Princess but is unsuccessful in his attempts to reach her.

The dance of the Princess and the Wooden Prince.

The loneliness of the Prince. His bitterness: Nature pays tribute to him.

The dance of the Princess and the Wooden Prince.

The Princess falls in love with the Prince but is unsuccessful in attempts to reach him.

The happy ending: peace is restored to Nature.

Bartók also referred indirectly to another organising principle in his score when he remarked that the first complete performance of *Two Portraits* gave him the impetus to re-start *The Wooden Prince*. The 'Faustian dramaturgy' of that score derives from Liszt's *Faust Symphony*, in which the musical portraits of Faust and Mephistopheles grow out of similar thematic material, although they are directly contrasted. Bartók created *Two Portraits* by pairing the first movement of the early Violin Concerto with a second piece on a similar theme; and he followed the same principle when composing the Second Piano Concerto, and the first and last movements of his late Violin Concerto. *The Wooden Prince* contains two variations on this idea.

Firstly, the themes of the Prince and the puppet are virtually identical, the puppet's theme being a distortion of the Prince's.

64

Secondly, when the puppet returns, exhausted, the theme of its first appearance is reversed, to express the 'inside-out' state of the puppet.

[2a]

[2b]

The opening music describes the cyclic renewal of Nature; it recalls a great operatic set-piece with a similar subject: the opening of *Das Rheingold*. Wagner starts the prelude with ascending arpeggios on the horns' natural harmonics to make a major triad as he whips up the waters of the Rhine. Nature begins to move in a similar way at the beginning of Bartók's ballet [3a], where the open notes are completed with F# and B*b* major to achieve a 'Nature chord' [3b].

[3a]   [3b]

Bartók inserted seven scenes in the ballet which he described as 'dances'. The first sets the character of the charming, capricious, mercurial Princess, with its semiquaver triplets and dotted semiquaver. There is a precedent in two pieces of the piano-cycle *Sketches: Portrait of a Girl* and *Swing-Swang*. This is the musical picture of the Princess:

[4]

65

The Prince sets off. Here the unison Myxolydian melody, reminiscent of a folktune, captures the mood.

[5]

It too has a precedent in Bartók's work — the *Peasant Song* of *Ten Easy Piano Pieces*. Moreover this sorrowful, pensive theme [6a] was to return to support the fiercely ruthless, urban voice of the *Mandarin* [6b].

[6a]

[6b]

[6a] cont'd

[6b] cont'd

In the two dances which follow, the forest comes alive, and the river overflows. The sounds are disconcerting and inhuman: tritones on muted tumpets give the woods a gloomy atmosphere, worthy of Richard Strauss, and there is a frighteningly sombre waltz. Both dances also contain elements of more folk-like melody, such as the song of the receding waters in Dorian mode:

[7]

66

The Prince successfully conquers the forest but cannot pass through the river in flood. How is he to attract the Princess's attention? By making a puppet he partly recreates himself in a strange form, and it is ingeniously logical to use a musical device to express the unity of substance between him and the puppet. The Prince's 'work-song' is as cheerful as Siegfried's song when he hammers out his new sword.

[8]

Apparently the Prince achieves his goal, for the Princess runs out of her castle to see the puppet. But she is interested in this strange spectacular creature and not in its creator.

By magic, the Fairy brings the puppet to life. We recognise its grotesquely clumsy movements from the first part of the *Three Burlesques* for piano, and they will reappear in the old Beau's dance in *The Miraculous Mandarin*. The fourth dance begins: the dance of the Princess and the Wooden Prince. It is the first scherzo, but it is neither gay, nor even straightforwardly grotesque. The Wooden Prince's music is related to that of Hagen in *Götterdamerung*, and it suggests that for a moment the puppet becomes the cosmic arch-enemy, a terrifying force for destruction in the natural world.

The tale reaches a crisis when the Princess dances off with the Wooden Prince. Robbed of all his hopes, illusions and his crown, the Prince gives way to despair. His only way out is to dream. Nature, so recently an obstructing force, comforts him — perhaps only to try his strength again. It adorns him with its most beautiful decorations, and pays him homage. This slow middle movement is the emotional peak of the ballet: the poet is triumphant, king in the realm of his dreams.

From this point the musical sequence is reversed. The scherzo returns in distorted form when the Princess dances back with the now-exhausted puppet. During the fifth dance the Princess loses her infatuation for the Wooden Prince, the symbol of all that is superficial. She sees the Prince, 'standing in the brilliant light', and starts her seduction play in the sixth dance. It includes a musical reference to another of Bartók's early works, the scherzo of the First Orchestral Suite, and the clarinet solo is a forerunner of the seduction music in *The Miraculous Mandarin*. The Prince, his heart almost breaking, rejects her advances. During the seventh dance, the forest stops the Princess from running to the Prince. In despair she throws away her adornments; and this is how the Prince prefers her, without her crown and her robes, just as herself. The Princess's elegant music alternates with the Prince's quaint theme, and their love is triumphantly confirmed in Hungarian folk music. Peace is restored to Nature, and the introductory music returns. The picturesque story is over.

'The Wooden Prince': Performance History

John Percival

The Wooden Prince had its (unexpectedly triumphant) première on May 12, 1917, at the State Opera, Budapest — the only one of Bartók's stage works to be produced without a long delay. The choreography was by Ottó Zöbisch, assisted by Ede Brada, who danced the role of the Fairy. Little is known of Zöbisch, none of whose work survives. The Prince was played *en travestie* by Anna Palley, with Emilia Nirschy as the Princess and Boriska Hormat as the Wooden Prince.

An unsuccessful attempt by M.D. Calvocoressi to interest Diaghilev (who had earlier employed him as an assistant) in *The Wooden Prince* for his Ballets Russes produced the comment, after an inspection of the score, that it was 'false modernism'. In fact the ballet has never retained a place with any ballet company outside Hungary, nor has it been staged by any of the world's leading choreographers. The best regarded of the many productions in Western Europe have been those of Aurel von Milloss (Venice, 1950) and Erich Walter (Wuppertal, 1952).

In Hungary the work has enjoyed more frequent production, despite the hiatus after 1919 when Balázs was out of favour because of his connection with the short-lived communist regime. Jan Cieplinski mounted a new version in 1935, and there was another in 1939 by Gyula Harangozó, for more than 25 years one of the most important figures in the Hungarian Ballet as dancer and choreographer. Ernő Vashegyi made a version in 1952 but Harangozó restored his in 1958. László Seregi, whose *Spartacus* (1968) established him as the leading choreographer of the Hungarian State Ballet, followed that in the same year with versions of both Bartók ballets. Imre Eck, founder-director of the Ballet Sopianae in the city of Pecs, mounted *The Wooden Prince* there in 1965.

The Budapest productions of the Bartók triple bill have toured: Harangozó's production was brought to the 1963 Edinburgh Festival, and Seregi's to the Royal Opera House, Covent Garden, in February 1989. The only British production was also part of a triple bill given jointly by English National Opera and London Festival Ballet at the London Coliseum in 1981. Geoffrey Cauley was the choreographer and Philip Prowse the designer. The ballet was never repeated outside that context, and these three productions, totalling about a dozen performances, have been the only ones given in Britain.

*

The ballet was inspired by this scenario, first published in the magazine *Nyugat*, in 1912. A comparison with the ballet synopsis in Ferenc Bónis's preceding article will show that there are significant differences in Bartók's plot, which is divided into seven dances and obscures the dramatic significance of the Fairy's role. This translation first appeared in *The New Hungarian Quarterly*, and was reprinted in *Bartók Studies*, 1976.

The Wooden Prince
A fából faragott királyfi

A Ballet in One Act, op. 13

by Béla Balázs

Scenario by Béla Balázs

Translation by István Farkas

Fenö Löcsei as the Prince and Edit Szabadi as the Princess in the Hungarian State Ballet's 1989 production choreographed by László Seregi. (photo: Béla Kanyó)

CHARACTERS

The Prince	The Wooden Prince
The Princess	The Forest
The Fairy	The River

69

The Scene

A grotesquely primitive setting. Downstage left, there is a hillock. A tiny castle is perched on top of the hillock. It's a turreted toy castle, with its outer wall removed so that the interior is laid open to view — the kind one sees in charming old Italian paintings. We see a small room that contains a table, a chair and a spinning wheel. (This is about all it can contain.) We notice, in the right wall of the room, a small window overlooking the country below, and, in the wall at the back, a little door. (One cannot help wondering how a tallish person can possibly squeeze through it.) There are two flights of stairs leading from the exquisitely beautiful castle. One curves down this side of the hillock. The other barely shows on the far side. It obviously snuggles up to the threshold of the little door at the back, prostrating itself reverently before it.

The little hill is girdled by a streamlet. You shouldn't assume though that this is some turbulent, choppy, shapeless body of water — no, silvery-blue wavelets, large, tender and round, are ranged in it peacefully, showing up in candid self-exposure, like the breasts of a hundred women reclining. The near path curves across them over a bridge. The silvery-blue circle of the streamlet is ringed by the black-and-green hoop of a pine-wood. It is a vast forest, to be sure. The trees stand in rows, four deep, motionless and still. For here there is no rumpled, scrubby brushwood. From the open arms of the trees heavy green curtains are dropping, trim, one like the other, as though they were rigid lines of well-groomed ladies-in-waiting trying to hide and shield something.

A road leads from the forest into the open country (to upstage right). A big boulder lies by the roadside (down centre). Up centre, there is another hillock, crowned by another little castle. The road runs right up to the gate, which is shut — they don't let it run any farther.*

Beyond that, nothing is seen, only a golden sky. And everything is plain and orderly. This is a world where Things have made a covenant and are at peace among themselves. They have nothing against each other any more. They have spoken their last word and are now waiting for Man to give his final answer.

First Dance

Opening music sounds while, slowly, the curtain rises. Everything is plain and orderly, the music says, and things are at peace. However, the music also speaks of some great and silent, harrowing desire, for in this peace Things have spoken their last word and are now waiting for Man's reply. It's a long, dismal waiting. The curtain is up. As our eyes follow its rise, we behold, near the apex of the set, at the foot of the nearer castle, a tall woman sheathed in a grey veil. She is standing motionless, gazing afar, toward the further castle. Yet the grey veil falls over her face too. There is about her an air of suffering (could it be the suffering of that waiting?), of mystery and of terror. She obviously is not human, and yet one cannot help feeling a fondness for her.

Down below, at the foot of the hillock, in the middle of the forest, the little PRINCESS is at play. Her golden hair is topped by a gold coronet, a silver mantle hangs from her slight shoulders. Flowers in hand, she dances round the trees in wide-eyed wonderment. They do not stir. With nimble, coquettish and capricious movements she skips about among the trees. She is so lonesome and would like to make friends with the trees. But they do not stir.

---

* *Roads have a tendency to surge into houses; but people shut them out. Roads are dangerous enemies of peaceful hearths. — The Author.*

Second Dance

The music grows restless. Something is going to happen. The GREY FAIRY stirs: with her arms she draws marvellous, sweeping arches over the country. 'Attention! All set — Now!'

At that, the gate of the further castle opens and there emerges from it the PRINCE. His curly golden hair is topped by a coronet, and a purple mantle drapes his broad-shouldered back. But, oh, he has a haversack slung over his mantle, and in his hand he grips a staff! It is a big walking-stick as tall as himself. Obviously, the PRINCE is off to see the world.

The PRINCE waves goodbye towards the slowly closing gate.

After that, he advances a few steps downstage. He opens his arms: 'Oh, how beautiful, how wide the world!' He comes capering down the slope. 'Oh, to go rambling — how wonderful!'

The GREY FAIRY, leaning forward, watches the PRINCE as he approaches with gay, dancing steps. 'So there you are. So you're coming at last. I have been waiting for you so long.' She then comes down the hill. Her movements are fraught with mystery and majesty. She crosses over the bridge and enters the forest, where the PRINCESS is engaged in her child-like dance, not suspecting a thing.

The PRINCESS makes an endearing curtsey before the FAIRY OF THE GREY VEIL and ingratiatingly dances around her also.

The FAIRY OF THE GREY VEIL sternly points towards the castle: 'Get back up there! Go home! Get along with you!'

The PRINCESS, sulking: 'I won't! Why should I? I just won't go!' Suddenly she skips away like a cat and dances off. 'Catch me if you can.' The FAIRY opens her arms, from which veils are flowing like two grey wings. She seems to fly on them after the PRINCESS. She catches up with her, and drives her away with magic movements of her arms.

The PRINCESS, whimpering, runs for the bridge and, sulking and crest-fallen, goes slinking up towards the castle. But she turns about, scowling: 'You'll pay for this. Just you wait.'

The FAIRY OF THE GREY VEIL keeps glancing back at the PRINCE, who is coming up the road, as she shoos away the PRINCESS. Her intention is quite obvious — she does not want those two to meet. While the PRINCESS, with bowed head, climbs up the hill, the FAIRY turns about, walks up to the edge of the forest and, with her arms wide open, greets the PRINCE as he arrives there. What is she up to? Surely she isn't trying to show herself off?

The PRINCE is about to reach the edge of the forest when he perceives the FAIRY appearing in front of him. He stops in his tracks, amazed. Who is this? What is this?

The FAIRY OF THE GREY VEIL stands still, while a soft rocking starts from her hips and goes rippling up over her body to her finger-tips. Is it a summons? It is a sweet summons if you understand it. If you don't, it is a frightening enigma. The PRINCE is puzzled and shrinks back in dismay. But it seems as if he were with much difficulty pulling his unresponsive limbs out of some magnetic current. And what happens now? As he comes to the edge of downstage right he glances up towards the hill and catches a glimpse of the beautiful PRINCESS who is about to enter her palace. And, bang, he falls in love with her on the instant. He runs forward, he runs right, he runs left — he doesn't know which way to run. He flings his arms open, goes down on his knees, then jumps to his feet as if to take wing. (One wonders, indeed, how such a whirlwind love — listen to the music and say so — can fail to snatch him up and precipitate him through the air.) His dance expresses a desire that makes him toss and writhe. As if he were tugging at fetters that bind his limbs. As if he felt shackled by his own body, by the world at large! The PRINCESS has not noticed him. She has no idea that the PRINCE is already there.* She knows nothing; and so she enters her little castle (whose interior is so agreeably exposed to view), seats herself at the spinning wheel near the window, starts the wheel, and begins to work. (Working at this time of day!)

The FAIRY OF THE GREY VEIL has seen what happened only too well. Impossible not to see it. The PRINCE wants the PRINCESS, and wants her badly. The tall figure of the FAIRY bows, she folds her arms over her head and withdraws into the forest, passing over the bridge and up the hillock. Why should it hurt her so much? What can she have been expecting? The music conveys some sadness . . . And up there, in the castle, the spinning wheel is whirring away.

Third Dance (Grand ballet)

The PRINCE jumps up. 'I'll go up to her. It's the simplest thing to do.'** And he runs off, exultantly, towards the forest. But lo! even as he is about to enter it, what happens?

The FAIRY OF THE GREY VEIL draws magic circles with her arms. It's a command from a haughty and mighty person. And behold!

The FOREST stirs into life! The music now speaks like an eerie wind, and the trees sway to right and left, pointing their branches at the PRINCE. A marvellous sight! The trunks are swaying like supple female bodies, and the branches are swinging like the slender arms of women, and the foliage flutters like so many green veils. The trees seem to have turned into women. The PRINCE recoils, taken aback, and for a moment changes his mind. But he looks up at the castle. 'There's the Princess I've got to get up there by any means!' After all, he is a prince and he will not take fright at a living forest. He lays down his big walking stick and makes a determined dash for the trees. But see what happens now!

The FOREST moves! Four lines of trees, like four dancing whirlpools, swirl around the hillock. How will you get through here, oh Prince? And so the dance struggle is on. The PRINCE dashes against the magical dancing forest and rebounds from it. He repeats his charge once, twice. Now he has got through the first ring of trees.

The FOREST's outermost ring of trees has stopped, as though petrified. The spell has been broken. Yet three more rings of trees are still swirling round the little hillock. The outermost danced most slowly of all.

The PRINCE finds this a kind of tag game. The dancing starts anew. He now finds it more difficult to get through between the trees: here, the roundelay goes faster, the whirl is swifter. Still, at one place, he manages to slip through.

The FOREST reveals that two of its rings of trees have already stopped. The trees are standing still, only their tops continue swaying. Is it because they

---

* That is always the source of trouble. Princesses ever hang back till they can see a thing with their own eyes. But by then the best part of it has been lost. That's how it is. — The Author.

** This thought, as a rule, does not at once suggest itself to princes in love — real-life princes, that is. — The Author.

cannot stop their motion on the instant? Or do they mean to say, 'It's no use. No. No. No. No!' We shall see.

The **PRINCE** is very clever, to be sure. He has negotiated even the third ring of trees, which stand behind him wagging their tops. But the fourth ring! That's a different matter! Like dry herbs blown by the wind, like raging witches, the trees toss and swirl in front of him. But the **PRINCE** is not to be outdone. He is tossed and spurred on by love. Oops! He's got through, and has now come to the bridge. What now? He starts for the bridge. Now he is about to set foot on it.

The **FAIRY** — who has been watching the scene from on high and performing wonderful gyrations with her arms and body as though she was driving those trees round and round in whirling rings as a ringmaster drives his manege — now, for the second time, makes a sign in magic command. And lo!—

The **RIVER** rises in its bed, and its silvery-blue waves lift up the bridge and toss it backwards, against the slope of the hill. (Now, my Prince, there's a dance for you! A dance of the waves!) Silvery-blue veils float and flutter and stream. It is as though they were the undulating bodies of a hundred women. Perhaps they really are?

The **PRINCE** once again shrinks back. But he is not the sort to give in. He runs up and down the river bank, but this time to no avail.

The **RIVER**'s dancing, undulating ring of babbling, rippling waves leaves no loophole. Indeed, the trees behind the **PRINCE** are still saying, 'No! No! No!'

The **PRINCE**, tired and beaten at last, slinks back through the trees, whose tops are still swaying, saying no. He walks back to where he laid down his staff and picks it up sadly. (My god, how very sad he is!) No use — the **PRINCESS** cannot be reached. With his head hanging, he starts off to right. The **FOREST** and the **RIVER** have stopped, and the bridge is now back on its pillars, spanning the river.

The **PRINCESS** — what has she been doing all this time? Why, she's been pushing the treadle and spinning the spindle. She's been doing nothing.*

She did not even know that the **PRINCE** was down below.

Fourth Dance

The **PRINCE**, however, turns to look once more. He cannot possibly go away without taking just one more look. He opens his arms: No, no, it is impossible to give her up, impossible to tear oneself away from her! He turns back. Again he starts for the forest. He stops dead — it's useless that way. 'My god! My god! What shall I do?' He can see the little gold coronet through the window of the castle. 'There she is! Oh, if she would but lean out and look down! If she but knew that I am here! How can I make her notice me?' He leaps high, stands on tiptoe — all in vain. Suddenly, an idea flashes through his mind. He takes off his coronet and turns it round, looking at it affectionately: 'This is my glory, my emblem and ornament. You shall announce to her my presence.' So he hangs his coronet on the head of his staff, climbs on the big boulder, and reaches the coronet up high. He waves his staff, 'Halloa, Princess!' The **PRINCESS** looks up. She sees the coronet beyond the window and eyes it with curiosity, but without stopping her work to do so. After taking a good look at it,

---

* Indeed, there is nothing wrong about princesses not helping princes in trying to win their hearts. — The Author.

she pores over her wheel and goes on spinning the spindle with indifference. The music imitates a derisive, scornful humming. The **PRINCE** lowers the staff with the coronet. He grows excited, pricks up his ears. He feels sore: 'What! Isn't this coronet enough for her? She takes no notice of it? Yet there's no other coronet to compare with this one in all the world. Never mind. She *will* take notice of me. She must. If she ignores my coronet, I shall show her something else.' Thereupon he throws his fine scarlet mantle from his back and ungirds his sword. What is he going to do? In a trice, he ties his fine straight sword to the staff, crosswise, so that it looks like the skeleton of a scarecrow. Then he wraps his scarlet mantle around the sword and sticks the gold coronet on the staff. Why, now it almost looks like a real-life prince! If he were to plant it in the middle of a wheat-field, he might fool the birds. 'Now, my Princess! Look who is here.' He raises his coronet-topped, mantle-wrapped staff up high, proudly, triumphantly. This standard is invested with all his insignia, his regalia, and under it he is standing on tip-toe — a plain, unadorned fair-haired boy.

The **PRINCESS** sees the regalia. Now that's something. The wheel stops; her little head turns with interest towards the strange standard — but that is all. After a while, the sound of the wheel turning and the spindle spinning is heard again. The music imitates a scornful, derisive humming. The **PRINCE**, exasperated, lowers his crowned scarecrow. What'll he do now? He is fuming with rage. And that odious humming noise! 'That beautiful Princess up there cannot possibly remain quiet once she knows that it is I who am here below! Evidently the dummy is still a poor one. Imperfect. It is not invested with my beauty. It just isn't ME!' In a fit of exasperation, he opens his haversack and produces a big pair of shears. Now, what's he up to? Why — good heavens! — he is clipping off his fine, long golden hair! Then he takes the hair and arranges it as a wig on top of his stick and puts the coronet on top. But now the thing is the spitting image of the Prince! Seeing it from afar, his own mother would believe it to be her son.* Now then, he once again raises the wooden dummy. He does so neither haughtily nor with enthusiasm, just simply, as one will show one's best work to announce to the world: 'Look! Here I am!'

The **PRINCESS'** humming wheel stops instantly. She jumps to her feet, amazed: 'Oh! Isn't he good-looking!' She feels a rush of warmth to her heart. She is overcome with an emotion such as she never has felt before. She reaches her little hands through the window. 'He is the most handsome Prince I have ever seen. I must have him!'

The **PRINCE** exultingly flaunts the dummy and, hiding behind it, retreats with dancing steps, enticingly: 'You'll come down! You'll come down!'

The **PRINCESS** leans out of the window, alarmed: 'Is he going away? Oh, my God! I'll run after him.' She runs out on to the road on this side of the hill, but catches sight of the **FAIRY**. She runs back into her little castle and flings open the door at the back. However, before leaving the castle, she snatches up a little mirror from the table. 'Am I pretty enough? Will the handsome Prince like me?' She titivates herself like a kitten, gathering up her hair, which reaches to her knees, and lifting it on both arms as if to weigh it. After that, she slips through the door. The **FAIRY** — now what has *she* been doing all this time? She's been standing motionless, watching that queer **PRINCE** invest a wooden dummy with all his ornaments and beauty. But having seen him cut off his hair and, waving the Wooden Prince enticingly, go dancing off, she furtively

---

* Why, yes, that's what princes are like. They would strip off their skin to be able to make a true image of themselves — and no mistake. — The Author.

creeps down the slope of the hill and hides herself in the forest. Leaning forward she stares in front of her, on the watch like a beast of prey crouching before springing. What is she up to?

Fifth Dance (*Minor Ballet*)

The PRINCESS has also just come along the other path. She runs across into the forest and, smiling and coquettishly, dances towards the Wooden Prince, with whom the real PRINCE has reached the right-hand corner of the stage.

The PRINCE now draws himself up: 'At last! You've come at last!' He sticks the Wooden Prince into the ground (its back to the audience) and steps forward from behind it, with his arms flung wide open, proud and happy . . . But oh, what's this?

The PRINCESS, repelled and frightened, begins to flee from him. 'Who is that ugly, ungainly, bald man? What does he want of a Princess like me?' (Oh, poor young Prince, you have no coronet and no hair.)

The PRINCE still smiling, his arms still open, pursues the fleeing PRINCESS. 'Why, this is but a play of lovers.' (Oh, poor, poor Prince.)

The PRINCESS, her eyes fixed on the handsome Wooden Dummy, waves her hand at it and wants to get through to it, dodging, with dancing steps, the ungainly, bald man.

The PRINCE now understands. He bars her way! 'What do you want? Where are you dancing? Why, that is but a wooden dummy! All the ornaments you see on it are mine! All that is me! Me! Me!' (Oh, you poor Prince.) And the chase is on.

The FAIRY — as though this were the chance she has been waiting for, when those two in their dodging and chasing come to the centre of the stage, with the Wooden Prince standing, forsaken, backstage — comes out of the forest and runs across the stage to right, to the Wooden Prince, her grey veils fluttering ominously. Lo! Now she is treading softly round the dummy in a wondrous, magic dance. Is she casting a spell on the dummy? And now — look! look! — The DUMMY begins to stir. The mantle is waving lightly as if filling up with body. The wig quivers as if it had settled upon a head. And look! The dummy raises an arm. The music is now full of crackling and pattering sounds as of gnarled twigs being broken. The Wooden Prince stirs and moves. (If anyone should think that some leggy actor has shot up out of the trap and got into its frame — all right, that's none of my business.)

The PRINCESS notices that the dummy has stirred and joyfully waves her hand at it, calling upon it alarmedly: 'Come, help me! Let's get to each other! Look, this ugly, bald man wants to catch me.' (Oh, poor Prince.)

The FAIRY makes another movement — giving the dummy a push — and then goes stealthily back into the forest.

The DUMMY, the wretched thing, is moving! It is dancing — if that is the word — towards the PRINCESS. It moves as though its every limb were breaking as it bends them. Well, a dummy's a dummy — anyone can see that. With one exception. The PRINCESS sees only the coronet and the mantle, and the curling golden hair — the very things princesses want. Let him dance!

The PRINCE dances with fascinating grace and bewitching sadness; his very soul is moving in his limbs. But it is all in vain. The PRINCESS dances to right and to left. It is like a game of tag, and it goes on for a while. Now! She has reached her partner, after all. That Wooden Dummy! Well, she asked for it.

The PRINCESS joins hands with the WOODEN PRINCE and tugs away at him, trying to make him join in the dance. And he does dance, bless him — every splinter and chip in his body is cracking and creaking. In this manner they go dancing out.

Intermezzo

The **PRINCE** stands there forlorn, without mantle and coronet, bald, looking on as the beautiful Princess dances off with the Wooden Dummy he has made. And he watches the creation of his own hands, invested with his own beauty so as to make it a herald of himself, dancing with his loved one, who, he is sure, has been waiting for him and been looking for him and no one else*. Oh, poor young Prince! For you, it seems, the game is up. Already, the dusk of evening is gathering about you; the surrounding country is turning gloomy, heavy and grey. It's all over. The poor **PRINCE** sits down on a stone lying by the wayside and buries his bald head in his palms. Nothing stirs. The music only is speaking; it says: 'Wretched love. Contemptible princesses. A life like that isn't worth living.' Yet nothing stirs. For all that soared and hovered has now sunken to the depths. Truly, his sorrow is like a boundless, monotonous wilderness — the music pours over it like a stray wind. Long the **PRINCE** remains sitting in that posture, while a heavy night is descending upon him. Maybe it will even bury him.

Fifth Dance (*Grand ballet and apotheosis*)

But as the scene grows dark and darker, a sort of uneasy shudder passes over the countryside. The **FAIRY** emerges from the forest. Her grey veils seem to light up. She starts moving, beckons to right, beckons to left — apparently issuing orders in quick succession. A mysterious bustling and whispering surges up in the music. Every Thing stands where it stood before, and yet it seems as if each Thing has changed its form.** And now begins the **FAIRY**'s magic dance. Now it becomes evident that she is Queen over all Things at this place. At first, she circles slowly round the huddled **PRINCE** in a wary, wheedling, endearing dance: 'Now you are suffering. It is as it should be. Now you are turning away from Life. Now you are mine!' And she flits about like a will-o'-the-wisp, like a luminous magic bat. And whichever way she turns, the night turns ablaze with magic light. (The light of the moon must be like that, shining over the lunar regions.) And wherever she turns, a shudder passes over all Things, and they stir and respond in whispers. Once more she flits around in a faster circle, and the Things move and follow her. The green-veiled trees of the forest start off, and the silver-blue-veiled waves of the stream leave their bed. 'Come on, come on, come here, all of you. Come and gather ye round my sad Prince.' And the Things, forming a semi-circle, surge towards the bald-headed and unadorned, sorrowful **PRINCE** to pay him their obeisance. 'Come here, more of you! I want all of you to come here! Now he is suffering. Now he belongs to us!' And it seems as if the slope of the little hill were sliding: all the Things that were on it — flowers and bushes and stones — come rolling down it; but they do so noiselessly and meekly. And little imps and elves are turning up from nowhere. For if so many Things can move, every

---

* You have no idea how often this sort of thing happens to princes that make up wooden dummies. — The Author.

** This point needs to be explained. Such things take place every night. At night, objects take off their masks, and we see them do it, only we do not recognize them, as it is dark. All the same, we know that, at night, everything changes. — The Author.

Thing can. And the Things, paying their obeisance, dance round the bald-headed **PRINCE**. And now the **FAIRY** walks up behind him and, softly, in a motherly way, addresses him: 'Raise up your eyes, o Prince, and look about you.'

The **PRINCE** raises his eyes and lets his gaze travel around. 'Ah! What's this?' It is like an awakening from a sort of sleep-reality into the world of dreams. 'Where am I? How light my poor, anguished heart feels! Why, this is a different world! Where is my sorrow?' And he almost starts looking for his sorrow. Yet it is gone with the world that has gone.*

The **FAIRY** now steps in front of him: 'You are in *my* land, o Prince. This is my country here. Your sorrow is gone with the world that's gone.'

The **PRINCE**, as in a dream, takes the **FAIRY**'s hand. It is the way the dreamer and the sleep-walker move. 'Oh, strange Fairy, I've had such great sorrow.' And, with the passing, reposeful languor of sorrow, he places his other hand too in the **FAIRY**'s, and lays his head on it. The **PRINCE** has surrendered.

The **FAIRY** strokes his head and makes a signal to the Things: 'Pay ye homage to him! He is now our King.' All Things pay their obeisance and prostrate themselves. And lo —

The **FAIRY** takes a wonderful head of golden hair from the calyx of a flower and gently presses it upon the **PRINCE**'s head. Oh, this is more beautiful a hundred times than the one he has lost!

The **FLOWER** bows its calyx and dances off. **ANOTHER FLOWER** advances and holds its calyx under the **FAIRY**'s hand. The **FAIRY** produces a splendid golden crown and sets it on the **PRINCE**'s head. Ah, this is more splendid a hundred times than the coronet he lost!

The **GREAT MAGIC LILY** advances and from its bell-shaped flower the **FAIRY** produces a mantle of petals and hangs it over the **PRINCE**'s shoulders. She then makes a sign of command to her hosts. The **PRINCE** rises. Ah, he is more handsome a hundred times than his former self — now lost — ever was. Is it quite lost, one wonders?

All **THINGS** dance round the **PRINCE**, fêting him. The trees form into lines; the waves prostrate themselves before him as a solid path; and smaller flowers, imps and elves — a gay crowd of flitting outriders — run ahead of him, up the hillside. The wave-path and the lines of trees lead to the foot of the hill.

The **FAIRY** now takes the **PRINCE** by the hand and, walking on the waves, between the lines of bowing trees, leads him over to the foot of the hill, where the trees and the flowers flock around him, forming a live arbour. 'Here. This is your throne. You are now King here, King over the soul-comprehending.'

The **PRINCE** lets his intoxicated gaze travel over the scene: This is triumph, pomp and splendour! No more suffering, no more night.**

Sixth Dance (*Minor ballet*)

Thus, there is triumph and pomp and splendour, and the **PRINCE**, radiant, is standing at the centre of **ALL THINGS**, which are paying obeisance to him. And now, of a sudden, over on the other side (upstage right) there appears — the

---

* Now there, my Prince, you can see the use of the world of dancing. If the world is bad it ceases to exist. Everything will dance to the throbbing of your heart. But this is true not only in the theatre. — The Author.

** This point too needs to be explained. Darkness is a veil that hides things; but once things have revealed themselves, there is no more veil, and darkness ceases to exist. For the **PRINCE**, for instance, the night has been dispelled. — The Author.

PRINCESS, tugging at the Wooden Dummy; she tries to make it dance; and dance it would, that miserable — DUMMY, were it not so hopelessly out of joint by now. Its coronet is cocked at an angle, like the hat of a drunk, its wig has slipped back over its nape, and its fine scarlet mantle barely hangs from one shoulder. The WOODEN PRINCE has broken down and is stamping through a rather extraordinary dance. The PRINCESS, exasperated, is egging her sorry partner on. She is angry with it, and boxes and tries to straighten it. Maybe she even hates it already. But there is nothing to be done about it, since she has chosen this one. Now, as she is struggling with the DUMMY she enters the alley of firs at the end of which the resplendent real PRINCE is standing. And as she catches sight of him, she stops and stands agape. She pushes the wretched wooden DUMMY away from her, and it crashes and slumps to the ground. She smiles at the PRINCE and stretches her small hands towards him. 'This is the most handsome Prince, after all. I *must* have him!'* And she starts towards him in a coaxing, coquettish, flaunting dance.

The PRINCE notices her and clutches at his heart. He cannot help it — she *is* the real Princess, after all. Yet he makes a reproachful gesture of refusal: '*Now* you'd like to have me, wouldn't you? It's crown and mantle and hair that you want. So go to your dummy! There it is! It's lying over there. Go away! I don't want you.' And he turns away from her and walks upstage. The FAIRY goes with him, but not intimately, as before, not taking him by the hand. When the PRINCE clutched at his heart, she drew her hand away and stepped back, and now she seems to have wrapped herself up even more in her veils.

The PRINCESS grows alarmed: 'Oh, my God! Is the handsome Prince going away? Is he angry? I'll run after him.' And off she goes.

Seventh Dance (*Grand ballet*)

The TREES bend towards each other, like so many 'V'-s closing, barring the way of the Princess.

The PRINCESS dances round the inner circle thus formed, to get to the PRINCE. The TREES, however, put new branches in her way, and the mound and the PRINCE on top of it are separated from the PRINCESS by the asteroid pattern of intertwining V-letters. This is the same kind of tag game again. But the interlinked walls of the firs rise like a star-castle; and the dance of the waves meanders in between them.

Eighth Dance

The PRINCESS, tiring of it at last, buries her face in her small hands and runs off, crying (to downstage right). But here she stumbles against the lifeless form of the wooden DUMMY and almost falls over it. She views it in disgust and exasperation. She kicks its coronet: 'Is that the thing that deluded me?' She kicks its mantle: 'Is this the thing that turned my head?' She kicks the wig: 'Is this the thing I fell in love with?' Then, in her utter despair, she snatches her coronet off her head and dashes it against the DUMMY; she throws off her beautiful silver mantle. 'I don't want these things! Better to have nothing!' But she does more than this: she whips out the big scissors from her belt — no decent princess goes about without her sewing things! — and cuts off at her shoulders her wonderful golden hair that reaches to her knees. 'I don't want anything! If the Prince does not want me, so I may as well be poor and ugly, a

---

* Princesses think in such direct terms. — The Author.

despicable creature!' She then falls on her knees before the stone on which the Prince in his sorrow sat some time ago and throws herself on it, sobbing. (Poor little Princess! Anyone would now take her for a shivering, out-at-the-elbows little shepherdess rather than for a Princess.)

The **PRINCE** has found it impossible, after all, to preserve his equanimity behind his stockade of fir-trees. Still and all, it was with the utmost difficulty that he brought himself to turning his back on the **PRINCESS**. Something makes him tingle all over, and he emerges from the forest upstage. He himself does not know what he wants to do — just saunters along, to the tune of some sweet music. As he advances downstage his eyes fall on the sobbing **PRINCESS**. Well, well, she isn't the haughty, coquettish Princess any more — she has shed all her ornaments. She has humbled herself.

The **PRINCESS** suddenly jumps to her feet. Her first impulse is to hide herself — it seems as if she wished to hide herself behind her little palms. She feels ashamed: 'Oh, I am ugly and deprived of all my adornments. He will abhor me. No, no, I'd rather not let him see me anymore!' And, turning her face away, with mincing steps, she retreats to the farthest corner upstage, where she crouches shivering. The **PRINCE** follows her nonetheless. 'When you came to me haughty and wearing your coronet and mantle and reached your little hands to me, I turned my back on you. But now you have humbled yourself and are like a poor shepherdess — now I will wrap my mantle around you and clasp you to myself.' And he does just that. He bends over the crouching **PRINCESS**, wraps his mantle around her and lifts her up to himself.

The **FAIRY** has been following the **PRINCE** in dismay and warily, as though she had a foreboding as to the end all this is coming to. And upon seeing the way the **PRINCE** approached the **PRINCESS**, the way he bent over her, she cut sweeping circles in the air with both arms in a flourishing of wailing and lament: 'Go back! Go back, my hosts! All is lost!'

ALL THINGS withdraw. The trees retreat to their place and the waters to their bed. 'Go back! Go back! It's been all in vain! Man has deserted us and gone back to Man.' And as the **PRINCE** has reached out his hand to grasp Life elsewhere, the Things again hide themselves in their state of benumbed lifelessness. And as the curtain slowly falls, the world resumes its simple, ordinary aspect. It again becomes ordinary and simple like the last word the Things have spoken and to which they are waiting for Man's ultimate reply. They are still waiting.

The **FAIRY** too has retreated to the hillock, her place of watch since long, long ago, and leaning forward, stands motionless, staring in front of her.

The **PRINCE** and **PRINCESS**, however, gaze at each other, and respond to each other, and are no longer concerned about the Things.

Curtain.

Michael Somes as the Mandarin in the Royal Ballet's 1956 production choreographed by Alfred Rodrigues, 1956. (photo: Houston Rogers/Royal Opera House Archives)

'The Miraculous Mandarin':
The Birth and Vicissitudes of a Masterpiece

Ferenc Bónis

The conception of the work — both libretto and music — is shrouded in mystery. The latest research offers a guide through the maze of often contradictory data and interpretations. Menyhért Lengyel's 'pantomime grotesque' was published in the January 1, 1917, issue of *Nyugat* (West), a Hungarian literary review, with a focus on the world as well as the arts in the age of Bartók and Kodály. *Esti Ujság* (Evening Newspaper), a 'well-informed' daily in Pest, claimed on January 17 that the novelty was not such a novelty after all, as 'Diaghilev, the director of the Ballets Russes performing in Budapest at that time, commissioned it from Lengyel, who did write the piece but was prevented from submitting the finished work to the director in the usual way by the outbreak of war.' This suggests that the idea for the libretto may have been conceived in 1912 when the Ballets Russes were performing in Budapest. The anonymous contributor also alluded, not very informatively, to the music. '*The Miraculous Mandarin* is awaiting the end of the war with miraculous patience. Meanwhile a composer of European fame, who is reluctant to shed his incognito is setting it to music.' Even the popular press in Pest, which was always inclined to exaggerate, would not have referred to Bartók in such terms as early as 1917. The writer must have meant Ernő Dohnányi, who had been taking an interest in the pantomime genre since 1910, in order to help his wife, Elza Galafrés, who could not speak Hungarian, to find work on the stage. In her memoirs, published in her old age, she maintains that Lengyel first offered *The Miraculous Mandarin* to Dohnányi:

> He, however, could not undertake to set it to music. First, he had two of his operas unfinished. Second, and this was the main reason, he thought that the theme of 'grand guignol' better suited Bartók's style [?!]. Bartók accepted the subject when it was offered to him. Later he showed his score to Dohnányi, who tried to draw his attention to what he thought was a flaw in the overture. In Lengyel's libretto the first scene was set in Paris. Bartók's music, however, struck an exotic note right from the beginning, thereby creating, prematurely, an atmosphere which should have been manifest only after the appearance of the Mandarin, representing his mysterious character and an alien world.[1]

Since Bartók's opening music is in fact permeated by the atmosphere of the metropolis, and we know that this was his idea right from the outset, there must be a mistake. It is inconceivable that Dohnányi would have made this remark, or objected to the lack of a feature which was very much present in the score. It shatters our confidence in the reliability of Elza Galafrés' recollections and casts a doubt as to whether Dohnányi ever saw the libretto. All the more so because the chief witness in this case, namely Menyhért Lengyel, never mentions Diaghilev, Dohnányi, the Ballets Russes nor any initial inspiration for the pantomime story in 1912. In a brief diary entry for July 5, 1919, which he did not intend for publication, he wrote only that, 'I wrote this pantomime tale in 1916, without any express purpose and it appeared in the New Year's Day issue of *Nyugat*'.[2]

Lengyel was writing after a memorable musical event. 'The other day Béla

Bartók played on the piano the music of *A csodálatos mandarin* (The Miraculous Mandarin) [...] to us in the flat of a mutual friend, Professor Thomán. Only Thomán, his immediate family and the two of us were present. What marvellous music! What a talent!'[3]

How did the paths of Béla Bartók and Menyhért Lengyel cross and how did the composer hit upon the pantomime story? It was previously supposed that 'Bartók read Menyhért Lengyel's libretto in *Nyugat* and it appealed to him so much that he approached the author by letter and asked to be allowed to set it to music. Lengyel readily gave his permission.'[4] A recently discovered document, however, puts the matter somewhat differently. It suggests that whether it was Bartók or Lengyel who took the initiative in setting the *Mandarin* to music, it was certainly through the mediation of István Thomán, a former piano teacher, and the composer's patron and friend. Thomán's postcard to Bartók — we know its content from a communication by Béla Bartók Jnr[5] — may be interpreted as the writer's agreement in principle to the composer's oral query, or as his wish to have set it to music.

On March 28, 1918, Thomán wrote to the composer in Rákoskeresztúr, a suburb of Budapest, addressing the letter to 'Béla Bartók Esq., music academy professor':

> Menyhért Lengyel would be delighted if you set the *Mandarin* to music. Please let me know when you are coming to dinner — I'd like to invite him also to meet you.

Two months later, on May 24, Lengyel, now Bartók's future collaborator, attended the first night of *Bluebeard's Castle*, the composer's first work for the stage, but the second to be performed. In a diary entry on the following day, he wrote:

> A first night. An evening in the Opera. Bartók's *Bluebeard's Castle*. I am as knowledgeable about music as anything else; for example, I admired Van Gogh and Cézanne at an age when I hardly had a notion about painting. I instinctively felt what real values were. Music can excite me so much that it exhausts me. I felt this last night too. I looked around in the theatre. Did they know that genius was present? Absolute genius, which dissolves the message that we, ordinary people, have to express in words. How shall I convey that the sun is shining outside? If I use too many words, it will be forced. I'm lucky if I find a new epithet because words 'go the way of all words' and get worn out with overuse, and you don't have to be a poet to replace hackneyed words by fresh ones; it's only a question of a little ingenuity and resourcefulness and you'll be regarded as a good writer. But all this is utterly incapable of conveying the thrill of life, the tingle that is impossible to name, for that can only be done by the man of music! Perhaps no one can do it like Bartók. And what a sad fate this work has had! It was shelved for six years. How did they dare not perform it? By force of what law?
>
> Let's be careful and let's be tolerant. Let's take a good look at anything new. And if we are not receptive enough, let's trust finer ears.[6]

On this occasion also, Lengyel 'instinctively felt where the true values lay'. Perhaps just because he did not have an education in classical music, he preserved his objectivity and allowed the music to act upon him. It is remarkable that he compares the means that the writer and the composer had for expression — 'how shall I convey that the sun is shining outside?' — by referring, whether consciously or unconsciously, to a scene in the opera, namely the vertiginous moment when the fifth door is flung open, when a sudden burst of sound and light floods the cold and dark chamber of the castle. Lengyel, the born dramatist, had unerringly sensed the opera's emotional climax. 'This absolute genius', he summed up in his diary.

Lengyel's recognition of Bartók is all the more striking because he was himself regarded as a dramatist of European fame since the success of his play *Tájfun* ('Typhoon') in Budapest, Berlin, Paris, Turin and London, while Bartók's stage career had only just begun — and in the closed world of war-time Budapest at that.

On June 6, Bartók himself commented on the first night, saying:

the greatest success of this year for me does not lie in this but rather in the fact that I have managed to make a long-term contract with a first-class publishing firm. Universal Edition (Vienna) made a reasonable offer to me back in January. After lengthy talks, we finally came to an agreement on all points and the other day I signed the contract, whose terms stipulate that all my unpublished works as well as works I am yet to compose will appear in the next few years to come. [. . .] This contract is certainly my greatest success as a composer so far.[7]

Fifteen days after the letter was written, the composer and the writer, also referring to Universal Edition, agreed on terms for setting the pantomime to music. The contract has come down to us in Lengyel's handwriting and signed by both of them.[8]

Contrary to what has previously been thought, the contract was not immediately followed by, much less preceded by, the musical composition of the pantomime. Bartók badly needed some rest and, in addition, he was expecting an opera libretto from Sándor Bródy, a short-story writer and celebrated playwright. He spent the first half of July at Vészto, staying with his sister's family ('to put on some weight and to relax in general'). In the second half of the month he went to Belényes, where he had been invited by his Romanian friend Joan Busitia, a grammar-school teacher. There he had made a long folksong collecting trip. After a brief period at Rákoskeresztür, he travelled to Felsoszászberek, where he was entertained in style by Baron Kohner, a patron of the arts. He returned home to Rákoskeresztúr in late August and embarked on the *Mandarin* with great energy. 'Bródy did not send the libretto, so I applied myself to setting to music the script sent by Menyhért Lengyel', he reported to Busitia, his host at Belényes on September 14. But on September 5, he had already told his wife, who was holidaying at Vészto, about his first ideas for the composition, expressing unequivocally that this very first conception was precisely the big city atmosphere which Elza Galafrés said was missing from the opening scene:

I am now thinking about the *Mandarin* too. It will be hellish music if I succeed. The prelude before the curtain goes up is going to be very short and will sound like horrible pandemonium, din, racket, and hooting: the audience will be introduced to the apaches' den from the hurly-burly of the metropolis.[9]

For the next eight months, there is not a word about the music of the *Mandarin* in Bartók's correspondence. Instead, it is full of references to shortages of food

83

'The Miraculous Mandarin' at Covent Garden: design by Wakhevitch and choreography by Alfred Rodrigues, 1956. (photo: Houston Rogers/Royal Opera House Archives)

and fuel, the difficulties of getting enough paraffin oil and candles, and the events of the chaotic political scene: comments on the dissolution of the Austro-Hungarian monarchy, the bourgeois revolution and the proletarian dictatorship — now exuding confidence, now full of anxiety and worries. Last but not least he wrote about his health and illnesses. The devastating flu epidemic of 1918 did not spare him and, with a terrible twist of fate, the disease attacked his ears. 'I hear a musical note as a narrowed-down second', the patient wrote — he found it difficult to speak. The doctor, who was called from Budapest to Rákoskeresztúr, was accompanied by Kodály, 'should a man's assistance be needed'[10]. As the composer's eldest son, Béla Bartók Jnr, recalled later, 'my father, concerned for me, asked Kodály to be my guardian should the worst come to the worst.'[11]

It seems inevitable that Bartók should have been caught up in Europe's 'Dance of Death', and be sucked into the hellish vortex of the war. At first, he was only a worried and shocked observer. The loss of close relatives on the battlefields, the limitations imposed on his work of collecting folksongs and the fact that the surrounding world plunged into fire and blood, silenced his voice as a composer. Later he experienced great hardship, both physical and spiritual. As the fabric of the Europe he had known was destroyed before his eyes, as the Austro-Hungarian Empire collapsed, kingdoms disappeared and frontiers were redrawn, he himself almost died of the epidemic raging across the continent. In this light, Lengyel's horror play came increasingly close to reality, and reality ever more and more like some horror drama. This is the background of the composition of *The Miraculous Mandarin*.

The next time the work surfaced in the family correspondence was on May

84

14, 1919. The composer's wife wrote about it to her mother-in-law living in Pozsony (today Bratislava), packaging the simple working report in some colourful gossip: 'B. is almost ready with the pantomime and will perhaps soon start arranging it. Galafrés is very curious to know about it (as you may know, she has become a pantomime artist), as she would like to take the Girl's role. He will play them some of it as a foretaste but they won't like it, of course, though the name Bartók has been associated with success lately and this perhaps makes the bitter pill attractive. You see how malevolent I have become!'[12] Despite its 'malevolence', the letter is an interesting contribution to the contradictory nature of the artistic friendship of Bartók and Dohnányi and gives an insight into the aversion sensed in Elza Galafrés' memoirs.

On June 9, 1919, less than four months later, the Mrs Bartók of Rákoskeresztúr, in a single line of a long letter to the Mrs Bartók of Pozsony, told her of a new event in the composer's workshop: 'The new pantomime is ready. B. is now orchestrating it.'[13] Bartók added a few news items to his wife's letter about the uncertainties of political life in revolutionary Hungary. The composer devoted two sentences to his new work: 'Who knows when my pantomime, *The Miraculous Mandarin*, can be put on stage . . . Incidentally, Galafrés would like to take the Girl's role.' His words are permeated with pessimism: today we can understand why Bartók put the project aside.

If, in May 1919, he saw a bleak future for *The Miraculous Mandarin*, he had no cause for optimism after the turn of political events in the autumn, and the restoration of the Monarchy. Both his earlier stage works were immediately taken off the bill of the Hungarian Royal Opera House because their librettist, Béla Balázs, was labelled 'a communist emigré'. Although several directors fought for their revival, this became possible only fifteen years later (the Opera House would put on *The Wooden Prince* and *Bluebeard* in 1935 and 1936, respectively). Such treatment did not encourage him to hurry on with *The Miraculous Mandarin*.

On January 10, 1920, he gave a shocking account of his winter misery to Menyhért Lengyel. The writer, who had tried his luck abroad in the meantime, had inquired about the prospects of a new joint work, *Scheherezade*.

> The reason I didn't answer your letter earlier is that it took me a long time to bring myself to complain. But I cannot avoid complaining if it is a question of trying to explain why I wasn't able to work. We live in great misery. True, there are no material shortages now, but what there is, is beyond the reach of the likes of poor people like myself. As a result, my family and I have to spend the whole winter together in our smallest room, where I cannot even do arrangement. I don't have a single folio of the *Mandarin* score ready, so I cannot even contemplate working on *Scheherezade*. [. . .] my income is hardly enough to meet the only luxury we have, not going hungry.[14]

The Wooden Prince and *Bluebeard* were performed in Frankfurt on May 13, 1922. The event was a landmark in Bartók's career as it was the first time his stage works had been performed outside Hungary; they were, moreover, works that were banned there. The performance itself, conducted by Jeno Szenkár, was 'rather bad' in Bartók's opinion[15] but the management of the Budapest Opera nevertheless felt compelled to consider staging something by Bartók and, as the revival of the earlier works was not possible, they tried to secure the rights for a production of *The Miraculous Mandarin*.

A letter from Baron Gyula Wlassics, the chief director (October 1, 1923), makes it clear that this plan could not even get off the ground for lack of an orchestral score. Baron Wlassics begged the composer: 'please make a sacrifice and complete *The Miraculous Mandarin* and submit the work to us to enable us to stage it in the middle of the 1924/25 season at the latest.' If the 'evident obstacles could be removed', he said they would consider reviving the other two stage works.[16]

All this convinced Bartók that it would be worthwhile arranging the compositional sketch of *The Miraculous Mandarin* which he had shelved in 1919 — if not for the Opera in Budapest then for any West European theatre which might take an interest. He set aside the summer and autumn of 1924 for the orchestration. On June 5, 1924 Bartók let the management of the Hungarian Royal Opera know by letter that he had begun writing the score and that he intended to submit the first half around July 15, and the second half around September 15.[17] The work, however, took much longer than planned. Bartók was only able to announce that he had just finished *The Miraculous Mandarin* in the Christmas 1924 issue of *Neues Pester Journal*, a Budapest daily.[18] Even if not accurate to the day, we therefore know from a reliable source that his work on the orchestration started in May or June 1924 and was completed in the following November and December.

Once the music was finished, however, and the obvious obstacle to performance was removed, inherent obstacles emerged: the subject and the music, which posed great difficulties for both performers and audience.

Either Budapest or a German city was a candidate for staging it. On February 1, 1926, the composer opened negotiations with the management of the Opera in Budapest but they reached no agreement, probably because of 'moral considerations' entertained by the management or the ministry which supervised the theatre. The Budapest Opera made two further attempts to stage it (in 1931 and 1941) but neither resulted in a production. The first performance in Budapest eventually took place on December 9, 1945, with a considerably altered libretto — when Bartók had been buried for ten weeks in Farncliff cemetery. Bartók also had Berlin in mind for a production because, until 1924, Jeno Szenkár worked at the Berlin Volksoper and he had conducted the German premières of *Bluebeard's Castle* and *The Wooden Prince* in 1922. Szenkár would have been delighted to perform the pantomime too but he left for Cologne in the autumn of 1924. Otto Klemperer, his chosen successor, finally accepted a contract in Wiesbaden rather than in Berlin, though both Bartók and Universal Edition had cherished high hopes that he would conduct the piece. So they agreed that Jeno Szenkár, the original choice, should conduct the pantomime but at a different venue, Cologne. The first night was on November 27, 1926.

No more unsuitable venue could be imagined for the world première of this work. Hermann Unger's report in the newspaper *Musikblätter des Anbruch* said everything about the atmosphere of the evening:

> Cologne, a city of churches, monasteries and chapels, rendered immortal in Heinrich Heine's poems, has lived to see its first, true operatic scandal. Catcalls, whistling, stamping and booing which went on for several minutes, and did not even subside when the composer appeared, nor even after the safety curtain came down, and which swelled to shouting when the composer and the conductor stepped out of the little door in the safety curtain, must mean something for us [. . .] The press, with the exception of the left, protests, the clergy of both religious denominations hold meetings [. . .], the Mayor of the city

[Adenauer, later Federal Chancellor] intervenes dictatorially and bans the pantomime from the repertoire [. . .] The waves of moral outrage strike high . . .

The scandal in Cologne decided the fate of the work in the theatre, at least while the composer was alive. He did not see the work on stage again. He was not present at the première in Prague on February 19, 1927, and when Aurél Milloss choreographed it for La Scala, Milan, with himself in the title role, the Atlantic separated the composer from war-ridden Europe.

Objectively speaking, it is no surprise that the average opera-going audience of the 1920s should find the events repellent: it is the violent love story of a prostitute and a mysterious stranger, ending in death. But in 1919 Bartók himself described the story as follows:

Just listen, how beautiful the story is. In an 'Apache' den three thugs force a beautiful young girl to seduce men and to lure them into the den where they will be robbed. The first turns out to be poor, the second likewise, but the third one is a Chinese. The catch is good, the girl entertains him with her dance, the Mandarin's desire is aroused, his love flares up, but the girl recoils from him. — The thugs attack the Mandarin, rob him, smother him with pillows, stab him with a sword, all in vain, because the Mandarin continues watching the girl with eyes full of love and yearning. — Relying on her feminine ingenuity, the girl complies with the Mandarin's wish, whereupon he drops dead.[19]

How is this conception realized in the score? The musical form is novel, and different from that of *Bluebeard's Castle* or *The Wooden Prince*. The opera is divided into three parts: it starts and ends with the representation of darkness but at its climax, everything is suddenly suffused with light, *fortissimo*. The seven pictures that fit into the threefold structure are also linked through a Wagnerian leitmotif: that of blood. *The Wooden Prince* has a more complex and more organic repeated structure. It has a five-part musical form, in which the end corresponds to the beginning, the fourth part corresponds to the second part and the third part is the focal point of the score as well as its emotional climax. The structure of the *Mandarin* is in three parts, but with no reprise.

I	II	III
The plot preceding the appearance of the Mandarin: exposition	The scene of the Mandarin and the Girl: tension climax	The love-death of the Mandarin: redemption and resolution

The number three — just as in certain types of Hungarian folktale or in the symbolism of freemasonry — is a key number in the work. The three thugs symbolise the forces of evil; the Girl lures the men into the den with three dances of seduction; at her call three victims appear and she starts three dances with them. Of the three men, it is the Mandarin who is the third, who suffers three murderous attempts from the gang until consummated love and death by love extinguish his desire and his life. 'Redemption' and 'death by love' suggest the world of Richard Wagner, which is not coincidental: the master of Romantic German music-drama exerted a greater and more lasting influence on the musical innovator of the twentieth century than one would at first think. Bartók's autobiographical First String Quartet (1908-1909) is an early example of the inspiration of *Tristan and Isolde*, for its dramatic span leads us from death back to life, with unmistakable musical quotations.[20] *Bluebeard,*

Lázsló Seregi's 1989 production of 'The Miraculous Mandarin' for the Hungarian State Ballet with Ildikó Pougor and Gábor Keveházi. (photo: Béla Kanyó)

like *Lohengrin*, is a story of the hopelessness of Man and Woman trying to find each other, abstracted from space and time. Both dramas turn upon a forbidden question, and the words and music of *Bluebeard* recall its Romantic predecessor. Of Bartók's three theatre pieces the folktale world of *The Wooden Prince* is the furthest from Wagner's mythical or historical landscapes — but its opening, the awakening of Nature, re-writes, as it were, the prelude to *The Rhinegold*, with its similar theme.[21] The music of the Wooden Puppet seems, for a moment, to evoke the fury of Hagen, the most evil character of the *Ring* cycle[22]. And if we can disregard the contexts — can we not perceive a modern version of Klingsor's wicked world in *Mandarin*, and the features of Kundry, the sinner who serves a higher cause, in the Girl? Does not the Mandarin, the envoy of an alien world, of Uncorrupted Nature, who encounters Sin, recall Parsifal and Amfortas: Parsifal, who brings Redemption through the power of love, and attended Amfortas, who cannot die until love has redeemed his sufferings? . . . Bartók visited Bayreuth in 1904, and attended a performance of *Parsifal*. He felt uneasy about the interminable prayers on stage but the scene of the Flower Maidens galvanised him. It is not surprising that the Girl's waltz in *The Miraculous Mandarin* echoes the Flowermaidens' erotic seduction waltz.[23]

Yet it is not these points of intersection with the past that primarily attract our attention in this score, but its striking novelty. In the words of the composer, one of its new features is its approximation to a certain kind of atonality. This 'certain type of atonality' involves the use of a powerful chromatic scale, although the use of ten notes of the twelve-note scale, in the thugs' music and in the Girl's seduction dances, never completely loses the ground of tonality. Another departure is the use of *ostinato*, so admired by Bartók in Stravinsky's music: the multiple repetition of rhythmic and melodic figures creates great excitement. A further novelty is the incorporation of folkloristic and exotic elements in the Mandarin's musical characterisation; these motifs had been vital elements in his art since the piano cycles of the *Elegies, Sketches* and *Funeral Songs*. These excited and exciting 'chase' rhythms had constituted his most characteristic forms of expression since *Allegro Barbaro, Piano Suite* and the fast movements of the Second String Quartet. The *Mandarin* contains hardly any traces of the post-Wagnerian elements of the orchestral sound in his earlier stage works. Stravinsky's direct or indirect influence is the more conspicuous: *Le Sacre du printemps*, with its 'neobarbarian' blocks and exciting *ostinato* just as much as his lesser works with their spacious, transparent arrangement. The acid test of Bartók's new, orchestral period is the *Dance Suite*, which he composed between the composition of *The Miraculous Mandarin* and its orchestration. Its peculiar tonality, its numerous innovatory string effects and the new writing for wind, in which *tutti* blocks are contrasted with solos, are marks of the progress in Bartók's practice of orchestration. They also served as preliminary studies for the *Mandarin*. It is as though everything that Bartók had tested in the more intimate forms of piano music and chamber music and, finally, in orchestral works, was preparation for the pantomime, and had a place in the overall context of a music drama without words.

The first major structural element of this music drama is the exposition, which lasts from the start until the Mandarin's appearance. Its introduction sets the scene, literally and psychologically — the city, which has become alienated from nature and everything that is natural, and which is the embodiment of evil, sin and inhumanity. The buzzing monotony of bustle and agitation is punctuated by the impatient and aggressive sound of honking cars. The 6/8 pulsation of this prelude is also the musical symbol of the three thugs living in the 'Apache' den: the depiction of the bustling and inhuman city is fused with that of the 'inhuman' thugs.

[1]

The curtain rises: the three thugs are looking for money. In vain. They order the Girl to stand in the window and lure men from the street, whom they can then rob. The root of the theme of the first thug (a) and the theme of the Girl (b) is identical:

[2a]

[2b]

[2b] cont'd

This indicates that at the beginning of the story the Girl unmistakably belongs to the world of the thugs. The first seduction tune is heard in the sensuous sound of the solo clarinet, which will later be repeated twice, in ever richer variations.

[3]

The first customer to be lured into the den, is a shabby-looking old Beau, the personification of superficial adornment (this is emphasised by the similarity of his dance to the music of the Wooden Puppet). He has no money, so he cannot be robbed. The thugs throw him out.

The second seduction tune lures a shy youth. His delicate, lyrical theme has an alien ring in the thugs' cruel, savage world. The oboe tune includes a motif, quite frequent in Bartók's works written after 1907, and called 'love quartet' in the literature:

[4]

The Girl starts a 'shy dance' with the youth: this is a character sketch unfolding in a 5/4 rhythm above the *ostinato* bass. The youth has no money either and the thugs throw him out. The Girl again begins her seduction tune, which marks the end of the exposition. We have now reached the focal point of the dramatic structure. Lured by her beckoning gesture, a wealthy-looking mysterious stranger appears in the person of a Chinese Mandarin, the representative of an alien world — the natural world.

[5]

His inscrutability is underlined by the way the harmonies of diminished fifths are associated with the pentatonic tune. The man is unresponsive, the Girl is scared and at a loss. Finally, overcoming her aversion, she begins her dance. The lilting waltz conjures up memories of the Flowermaidens in *Parsifal*.

[6a/b]

Wagner

Bartók

91

'In his feverish excitement', the Mandarin 'starts shivering': the development of his pentatonic theme (a) reflects his excitement (b):

[7a]

p *sotto voce, tranquillo*

[7b]

mf *sempre agitato*

[7a cont'd]

[7b cont'd]

'A wild chase starts and the Mandarin wants to catch the Girl, who is trying to get away from him.' The barbarous duet, with its hints of Stravinsky's *Sacre*, is the climax of the work (*The Miraculous Mandarin* concert suite ends with this scene).

[8]

Sempre vivace

f

In the final third of the work the drama takes a new direction. Instead of a repetition of the earlier actions, these are expressed in horrors: the triple murder corresponds to the three seductions in the exposition. After the thugs have robbed the Mandarin, they realise that they have to get rid of him. Brass, wind, percussion and low strings sound the Mandarin's death sentence. The thugs drag him to the bed and smother him with pillows. The sound of great sevenths heaped on one another marks the moment when they imagine that they have killed their victim. The Mandarin, however, does not die. His unfulfilled desire proves stronger than death. Then the thugs stab him with a sword, but to no avail. Now they hang him. But he cannot die in this way either. The minor third motif, sung by an invisible choir, wailing and without words, erupts from the depth of his soul as an expression of infinite suffering and a desire impossible to quell.

The Girl understands. She gestures to the thugs to cut down the hanged body. The Mandarin falls to the floor with a thud but springs to his feet and hurls himself at her. She no longer objects. Her waltz becomes intertwined with fragments of the chase theme. It is apparent that she has broken with the world of the thugs and sides with the Mandarin. They embrace, and their embrace has a cathartic force: the Girl is chastised through it and the Mandarin is redeemed from his desires and sufferings. 'His wounds start bleeding and he dies after a short struggle.'

What forces and extremes appear and clash in the score of *The Miraculous Mandarin!* East and West, past and present, pentatonality and atonality, Wagnerian redemption and Stravinsky's idea of barbarian sacrifice. No final synthesis is possible: uncorrupted nature cannot be reconciled with the civilisation of the rotten metropolis. Either the city subjugates nature or nature wins back from civilisation what can still be reconquered. The elaboration of this theme, however, will be left to another of Bartók's masterpieces, the *Cantata Profana*.

Notes
1. Elza Galafrés, *Lives . . . Loves . . . Losses*, Vancouver 1973. 2. Lengyel, Menyhért, ('The Book of My Life') Budapest 1987. 3. ibid. 4. Kroó, György, ('Bartók's Stage Works'), Budapest 1962. 5. Bartók, Béla, Jnr, ('The Chronicle of My Father's Life'), Budapest 1981. 6. Lengyel, op. cit. 7. Demény, János (ed.), ('Béla Bartók's Letters'), Budapest 1976. 8. Szántó, Tibor (ed.), ('In Honour of Béla Bartók'), Budapest 1988. 9. Bartók, Béla, Jnr (ed.), ('Béla Bartók's Family Letters'), Budapest 1981. 10. ('Memoirs of Béla Bartók Jnr') in Bónis, Ferenc (ed.), ('Kodály As We Saw Him'), Budapest 2/1982. 11. ibid. 12. Béla Bartók's Family Letters. 13. ibid. 14. Béla Bartók's Letters. 15. Bartók Jnr, *The Chronicle of My Father's Life*. 16. Demény, János (ed.), ('Béla Bartók's Letters. New Documents'), Budapest 1971. 17. Béla Bartók's Letters. 18. Ferenc Bónis, ('Six Statements by Bartók'), in Magyar Zene XXIX/4, Budapest Dec., 1988. 19. *Selected Writings of Béla Bartók*, ed. András Szöllősy, Budapest 1956. 20. Bónis, Ferenc, *Erstes Violinkonzert — Erstes Streichquartett*, Musica 39/3, Kassel 1985. 21. Bónis, Ferenc, *Bartók and Wagner*, Bayreuther Festspiele 1969, Programmheft VII, Bayreuth 1969. 22. Kroó, op. cit. 23. Bónis, *Bartók and Wagner*.

'The Miraculous Mandarin': Performance History

John Percival

The first performance of *The Miraculous Mandarin* was on November 28, 1926, in Cologne. Hans Strobach's staging appears to have obeyed the composer's description of the work as a mime play and to have been production rather than choreography; Wilma Aug and Ernst Zeiller took the leading roles. The subject, which had been the reason why no production was attempted in Budapest, was immediately banned for obscenity. A similar fate met a production in Prague the next year.

The stage history of *Mandarin* as a ballet effectively begins at La Scala, Milan, on October 12, 1942, with choreography by Aurel von Milloss, who was Hungarian by birth but worked mostly abroad. Milloss later revived it in Rome (1945), Rio de Janeiro (1954), Florence (1957) and Cologne (1961). The next recorded production, and the first in Hungary, was at the Opera House in Budapest on December 9, 1945, with choreography by Harangozó. It was soon withdrawn and disappeared until a successful revival in 1956. Seregi mounted a new version in 1970, which has remained in the repertoire, with minor revisions. A third choreography was provided for this company during the early 1980s by Antal Fodor as the middle section of his three-part ballet *Visions*. A young man, the hero of the first and third sections, took the place of the Mandarin, arriving on a motorbike from the auditorium and climbing onto the stage.

On March 26, 1989, the Hungarian State Ballet gave a unique performance consisting of these three versions: Harangozó's, Seregi's, and Fodor's (given outside its context for the first time). The company has since danced yet another version, by Milloss, as part of a memorial tribute to him. Harangozó's production toured to the Edinburgh Festival in 1963, and Seregi's to Edinburgh (1973) and Covent Garden (1989). Both the other leading Hungarian ballet companies, based in Pecs and Győr, have mounted the work, with choreography by their respective directors, Imre Eck and Iván Markó; the latter was brought to Sadler's Wells in 1989.

The first production outside Europe was given by New York City Ballet on September 6, 1951, with choreography by Todd Bolender. The first British choreographer to attempt it was Alan Carter, for the Bavarian State Ballet in Munich, 1955. In 1956 a production for the Sadler's Wells Ballet (shortly before it received its charter as the Royal Ballet) was choreographed by Alfred Rodrigues and designed by Wakhevitch; it opened at the Edinburgh Festival with Elaine Fifield and Michael Somes, but was dropped after only ten performances there and in London.

At the Bolshoi Ballet Leonid Lavrovsky altered the plot and produced it in 1961 under the title *Night City*. Of the many other productions in Europe, one of the most successful was made by Flemming Flindt for the Royal Danish Ballet in 1967, brought to Covent Garden in 1968 and revived for the London Festival Ballet in 1981.

Curiously, the only production of *The Miraculous Mandarin* to have had its first performance (September 6, 1970) in London was given in the studio theatre at The Place by the New Swedish Ballet from Gothenburg. The choreography was by Ulf Gadd and the music was recorded. Gadd revived this staging in July 1971 for American Ballet Theatre but, in spite of a cast headed by Natalia Makarova and Erik Bruhn, it did not endure.

The Miraculous Mandarin
A csodálatos mandarin

Pantomime in One Act, op.19
by Béla Bartók

Scenario by Menyhért Lengyel
Translation by István Farkas

Lengyel's scenario for a 'pantomime grotesque' was first published in *Nyugat* in 1917. This translation first appeared in *The New Hungarian Quarterly*, and was reprinted in *Bartók Studies*, 1976. Ferenc Bónis refers to a shorter version, which is included in the score.

The Royal Ballet's 1956 staging of 'The Miraculous Mandarin' designed by Wakhevitsch and choreographed by Alfred Rodrigues. (photo: Houston Rogers/Royal Opera House Archives)

CHARACTERS

Three Thugs
The Girl (Mimi)
The Old Beau (The Old Gallant)
The Youth
The Mandarin

The Scene

An upper-storey room: fantastic colours of squalor. Tattered wall-paper — bleak walls — comically crippled furniture — corners filled with odd things as in some shabby, disreputable old curio shop. In short: this is the den of three thugs, who use it as a store for stolen goods.

There is a door upstage with a window on either side. From outside, in a compound of vibrating street-lights and a mixture of confusing cries and noises, the life and hubbub of a huge city spill into the room.

1

MIMI and the three THUGS. The FIRST THUG is lying full length on the bed, the SECOND THUG is having a row with MIMI in the middle of the room. They have no money. He turns his pockets inside out — they're empty. The THIRD THUG eagerly rummages through the drawers of the dresser — nothing turns up. He too turns upon the girl. MIMI keeps shrugging her shoulders. Why can't they leave her alone? What do they want of her? It's not her fault. She can't help.

At this moment the FIRST THUG sits up on the bed: he is a big, grim-looking, reckless bully. He scrambles to his feet and walks up to MIMI. He grabs the girl's arm — and pulls her to him savagely. 'No money? Well you go an' get some!' MIMI, frightened, makes evasions: 'What am I to do?' The THUG: 'You go to that window and show yourself. Get someone to come up here — and we'll take care of him, the three of us.'

The two other fellows are all for the scheme. MIMI is reluctant — fists are raised to her face. The FIRST THUG pushes her brusquely to the window. Then the three men take counsel quickly: they're going to hide — one under the table, another behind the dresser, and the third concealed beside the bed. They do so, then wait.

2

MIMI at the window. She looks out; she waves her hand; she winks; she smiles — no result. Suddenly, she starts. Looks back timidly. The three THUGS poke their heads into sight: 'Got anyone?' She nods yes. The three men duck their heads again. They are waiting. Footfalls coming slowly up the wooden stairs. MIMI retreats to the middle of the room, her eyes riveted to the door, which now opens and frames — the OLD GALLANT.

He is a quaint dapper old man — tired, wrinkled face, but waxed moustache; shabby top hat; coat shiny with wear and ironing; suspicious-looking spats over what were once a pair of patent-leather shoes; dirty collar; cheap, gaudy tie; withered flower in buttonhole.

He enters smiling with the assurance of a gallant. After a few steps, he stops, looks the girl up and down. He is delighted. Takes off his top hat, places it on the table (hair, dyed and groomed with painstaking care, is smoothed over his skull), and, while eyeing the girl, begins to peel off his dirty gloves. MIMI stands still waiting.

Now the OLD GALLANT steps up to her and opens his arms, meaning to put them round her. MIMI takes a step back, looking at him inquiringly and, by rubbing thumb and index together, asks: 'What about the dough?'

The OLD GALLANT ignores the question — makes another amorous move. MIMI, now holding her hand close under his nose, repeats her question: 'What about the dough?'

The OLD GALLANT waves that aside; he smiles: 'Money — that's not important. It's love that counts.' He presses his hand against his heart — he is wooing her, showing off; he pinches her arm, her cheek, becomes increasingly fresh. MIMI, indignant, is hard put to it to keep him off when — the three THUGS spring forward and attack the OLD GALLANT. They form a chain from the table to the door, toss the old man from hand to hand and finally chuck him out the door. He tumbles down the stairs; and the thugs throw his top hat after him — one hears the hard hat roll tap-tap down the stairs. Resentment runs high among the occupants of the room. The old man is ridiculed, his wooing imitated. Once again the FIRST THUG confronts the girl menacingly: 'Mind you do it smarter this time!' Again he pushes her along to the window, and again the three men hide themselves. MIMI at the window: action as before — she swaying her hips provocatively. The frivolous music conveying temptation and whose volume has been gradually increasing, suddenly becomes charming, gentle and childlike, because —

3

MIMI has caught sight of someone in the street. She leans from the window, waves her hand and smiles. Then she turns about, clasping her hands joyfully. A gay, light patter of feet surges up the wooden stairs . . . the door flies open and reveals . . . the YOUNG STUDENT.

Rosy cheeks, blond hair, broad tie, short pants, big shoes. He has come rushing up to the door, but now he stops and stands helplessly, not knowing what to do with himself; he is panting, blushes deeply and casts down his eyes.

MIMI is studying him, smiling — he's a nice boy.

The STUDENT, smiling too in embarrassment, looks up at the girl.

MIMI beckons to him to step nearer.

The STUDENT advances timidly.

MIMI: 'Come here, little boy.' She takes his hand — how smooth it feels! She strokes his cheek — how rosy! His head — how blond! She draws him closer to her and again pats his cheek: 'You little darling. My, and how handsome and clean he is!' — She looks him up and down with delight. The STUDENT feels embarrassed and is awkward and sweet.

Now it strikes MIMI that this, after all, is but a victim, poor boy: she has got to try and find out what he's got on him. She puts her arms round him and light-fingeredly, quickly searches him. A glance at his hands — no rings; waistcoat-pocket felt — no watch; pockets of his jacket searched — there's only a handkerchief . . . She sniffs at it: it's scented! . . . She throws it away: Damn junk! Annoyed, she asks: 'Why, have you got no money at all?' The STUDENT sadly shakes his head. Depressed, despairing and helpless, he turns to go when — she takes pity on him very much: Poor boy. 'Come here, you little darling. No need to be sad like that. What a young boy . . . And how he's trembling . . . Come on!'

She throws her arms round his shoulders, caresses him, fondles him, mischievously pulls his ear, pats his cheek, then takes the boy's clumsy hands and puts them round her waist; they start waltzing slowly. Their movements gradually become more uninhibited . . . Cheeks begin to glow, their heads bow closer together — love burgeons in their hearts . . . The music grows more and more melting — they stop and look at each other, and laugh. They kiss.

At this moment, the three THUGS, who have been watching the scene with anger, jump out from their hiding-places, dash forward and pull the couple

97

apart. The boy puts up some resistance — but, of course, he hasn't a chance against those three bullies, and they throw him out the door. He has disappeared from sight, but down the stairs and through the courtyard and beyond, above the noises of the street, his sobbing is faintly heard.

In the room the ruffians turn towards MIMI; they are very angry. She is sorry for the boy and cries. The THUGS jeer at her: how is it that, of all the men she can have, she wants that little kid, that young nobody? Love, that's what she's after. And as if that's not enough, she feels sorry for him and goes and cries her eyes out for him.

The FIRST THUG draws his knife and threatens her: 'Take care — I'll cut you up! If you don't do something this time — if you don't get cracking — you're finished. Get back to the window!'

MIMI, trembling, obeys. Once again the three THUGS hide themselves.

The faint lament of the sobbing boy can be heard still, and back at the window, as she resumes her soliciting, the motif of temptation, of lust-provocation is heard again and works into a crescendo, suddenly acquiring a pungent, spicy, exotic colour.

4

At the window, MIMI starts. Alarmed, she takes a step backwards. The THUGS poke their heads forward: 'What's the matter?' She hovers at centre, dismayed and hesitant. The THUGS urge her to get back to the window, and timidly she returns to it. The exotic music increases in volume; the stairs are creaking. Her gaze riveted on the door, MIMI, trembling, retreats to the table. The door opens, and the MANDARIN appears on the doorstep.

A Chinese. Broad, yellow face; shining slit eyes — an unblinking, fixed stare like that of a fish. He wears a silk skull-cap, from under which a long black pig-tail falls on his back. He is dressed in a richly embroidered, loose-fitting yellow silk coat, black velvet trousers and very fine boots.

He wears a twisted, many-stranded gold chain around his neck, the buttons of his coat shine, and he has many diamond rings on his delicate fingers.

He is standing on the doorstep, looking at the girl with an unblinking stare, a deeply serious look in his eyes.

She is frightened of him and edges backwards. But whatever she backs into — the table, the dresser or the bed — the THUGS, from their hiding places, push her back toward the MANDARIN. At last she plucks up courage and cautiously approaches the Chinese, who is standing on the doorstep. She timidly invites him to come nearer. The MANDARIN does not budge. She invites him once again. The MANDARIN moves. Slowly, at a steady pace, he comes to the middle of the room. She points at the chair, motioning him to sit down. The MANDARIN sits down. But fixedly, unrelentingly, a darkly earnest look in his eyes, his set face never registering the least emotion, he continues to stare at the girl.

Something's got to be done at last, and MIMI, awkwardly and shivering, begins her show. She dances and whisks past the MANDARIN in a provocative manner. She waltzes round the room and as she comes to the door, with a sudden movement — always dancing — she bolts it, then dances on. The MANDARIN continues to watch her with his grave, unblinking stare. She dances faster and faster — by now she has thrown off some of her shyness, her movements grow less inhibited, and, as a spin brings her face to face with the MANDARIN, seeing the oddly stiff, unmoving posture of the Chinese, she bursts into laughter, which increases in force and, dizzy with the dancing, dissolving in laughter, plops upon the motionless MANDARIN's lap.

With the laughing woman lying, wriggling and tossing under his nose, the MANDARIN slowly undergoes a peculiar transformation. A soft tremor passes over him from top to toe. A blush rises to his cheeks. A flicker of his eyelids breaks his beady, fixed stare, and he starts blinking ever more rapidly. His chest heaves, his breathing becomes difficult and broken. His hands twitch, and his fingers — in increasingly rapid flits — wander onto her neck and head . . . His excitement mounts. Minute reflex actions burst forth — a twitch, a shudder passes over him — and a sudden hot rush of blood passing through him starts him shaking all over. The girl looks at him — and gets scared . . . She stops laughing, jumps to her feet and backs away.

The MANDARIN rises, too. He stretches his arms and moves towards her. She flees . . . The MANDARIN follows her, his eyes riveted on her, his face distorted and imploring like that of a sick animal.

The chase is on . . . The girl flits between the table and the chairs, with the MANDARIN intent on her trail . . . He leaps, makes a snatch at her, falls . . . Down on the floor, he manages to catch her by the ankles . . . She tears herself free . . . He jumps to his feet — his awkwardness and clumsiness are falling away from him . . . are gone . . . He moves with more alacrity . . . becomes extremely nimble and alarmingly grotesque . . . Now it is he who moves provocatively, starting to dance with fantastic movements. A strange, grating noise rises from his throat. MIMI grows increasingly frightened of him . . . She is fleeing, he follows in hot pursuit. He jingles his money and makes greedy snatches at her. He almost reaches her. She slips out of his hands. He is crying — tears streaming down his cheeks . . . He is completely beside himself — spinning, whirling, with increasingly alarming speed . . . He is now like a huge spinning top, fanning a whirlwind around him . . . His yellow coat and pig-tail stream through the air. It is impossible to avoid him . . . He catches the girl and with a rattle of intense happiness in his throat sinks with her to the floor.

At this moment the three THUGS rush forward and fall upon the MANDARIN. They hold him down and release the girl. They search his pockets — the gold coins fall from them with a jingle and roll all over the floor; they uncoil the long gold chain from his neck, pull the rings from his fingers. All this is done with lightning speed. Having plucked him clean, they exchange glances — and already the decision is taken to kill him. They grab him as if he were a parcel, throw him into the bed and on him heap pillows, blankets, mattresses, rags, everything, so as to stifle him to death. Pause. Then they make a sign at one another: 'Finished.' The girl is standing by the table, shivering. A slight pause. Then the THUGS sigh in relief: 'He's done for.'

At this moment the MANDARIN's pale, yellow head emerges from under the blankets.

It is a head with glassy eyes that start out of their sockets and are fixed on the girl.

The three THUGS are taken aback. The MANDARIN isn't dead! They pull themselves together. All right, let's finish him off.

They throw the blankets from the bed and pull the MANDARIN out of it. As soon as his feet touch the floor, the MANDARIN bounces up like some fantastic ball and hurls himself at the girl.

Before he reaches her, the THUGS catch him and hold him down. They twist his arms back, holding him fast. The MANDARIN, apparently unconcerned about what's happening to him, continues to stare at the girl with goggling eyes — two torches fed by the flames of a terrific inner fire.

The Royal Danish Ballet's version of 'The Miraculous Mandarin' with Flemming Flindt as the Mandarin and Niels Kehlet, Peter Martins, Flemming Halby as the Three Thugs, 1968. (photo: Anthony Crickmay)

The **THIRD THUG** produces a long and blood-stained, rusty knife. He motions to his two friends that they should hold the Chinese fast. Then, pointing the long knife ahead, dashes against the **MANDARIN**.

He runs the knife into the latter's belly.

The skin rips, the body slacks — the point of the knife emerges at the **MANDARIN**'s back.

They let go of the body and watch it fall — now he's sure to die.

For a moment the **MANDARIN** staggers, totters and stumbles — he is on the point of slumping (they are watching eagerly). Suddenly he regains his equilibrium, starts and jumps — and is at the girl again.

She flees, screaming.

Again the **THUGS** grab him and hold him fast. They too are alarmed and dismayed — all the more reason for doing away with him quickly.

One of the **THUGS** produces a big old-fashioned pistol. He aims it at the **MANDARIN**'s head and fires. Big bang and smoke. The **THUGS** jump clear of the **MANDARIN**. The smoke lifts — a dark singed hole shows on the **MANDARIN**'s forehead where the bullet passed through him. He staggers and totters — swings round and is once again at the girl.

He starts chasing her with grotesque bounds.

They seize him and hold him down.

This is something horrible. He has *not* died!

What is to be done?

Kill him! Kill him! You've got to!

But how?

One THUG points up at the chandelier.

That's where he's going to swing.

They lift him on a chair . . . they wind his pig-tail round his neck . . . And now one of the THUGS, standing on the table, strings the MANDARIN up on the chandelier by his pig-tail.The chair is kicked from under his feet — the MANDARIN is hanged.

The light goes out.

Darkness.

Silence.

Huddled together the three THUGS and the girl hold their breath in the darkness.

Suddenly a dim and eerie light looms up in mid-air.

The MANDARIN's rotund belly — like that of a Buddha, a fantastic sphere floating in the air — begins to shine.

The mystic light illuminates the whole figure of the man who has been hanged by his pig-tail — his big, yellow, round head, his eyes starting out of their sockets — eyes that, in a stubborn animal glare and with terrible desire, are turned on the girl like a pair of electric searchlights.

The THUGS, shuddering and a-tremble, scuttle for shelter; they creep under the bed and hide themselves.

The girl stays in the middle of the room.

She looks at the MANDARIN — for the first time without fear — and smiles.

She beckons to one THUG: 'Come here.' As the fellow refuses to go to her, she walks up to him and drags him along: 'You cut that mandarin down for me.'

The THUG dares not touch the man.

She urges him more energetically, putting the knife in his hand: 'I *insist* that you cut him down!'

At last the THUG, trembling, clambers onto the table, and with the knife severs the pig-tail.

The MANDARIN drops to the floor.

But again he rises and rushes at the girl.

She catches him in her arms. She hugs him and clasps him to herself in a long embrace.

The MANDARIN emits a rattle of happy fulfilment — he clings to the girl, and a tremor passes all over his body.

At this moment the wound on his belly and the hole on his forehead start slowly bleeding.

He is gradually fainting away; his hug slackens and his arms drop; his knees give way beneath him.

There is a happy look in his fixed stare, but slowly his eyes close.

A smile hovers on his contorted face.

His desire is spent.

Slowly the girl, triumphantly smiling, lowers the body on the floor — to the sounds of a quaint and strident, exotic music.

The MANDARIN is dead.

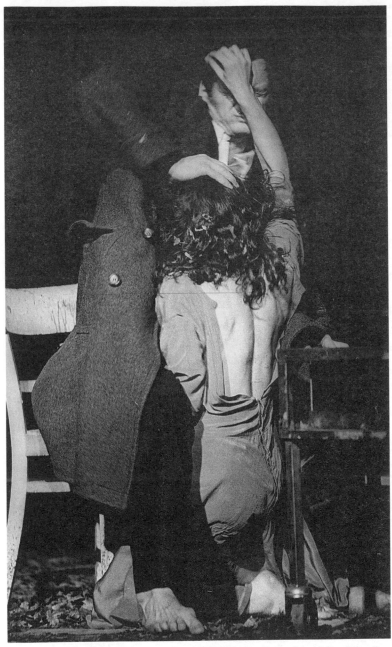

Pina Bausch's contemporary dance version of 'Duke Bluebeard's Castle' with Jan Minarik as Bluebeard and Beatrice Libonati as Judith. (photo: Ulli Weiss)

Bartók's Ballets

John Percival

When he died in 1945, Bartók would have had to be considered a failure as a composer for dance. Neither of his two ballets had established itself in the repertoire of dance companies, nor had choreographers begun to turn to his other music, as they were frequently to do after 1950. Even today *The Wooden Prince* is hardly ever seen except as part of a triple bill of Bartók's stage works, with the other ballet *The Miraculous Mandarin* and the opera *Duke Bluebeard's Castle*. It thus has the dubious distinction of being the only self-contained ballet (as distinct from opera-ballets) which is at least as likely to have been seen by opera-lovers as by balletomanes.

The neglect of *The Miraculous Mandarin* and *The Wooden Prince* may be partly explained by their plots, but also by a practical consideration. Both demand large orchestral forces beyond the reach of any ballet company without the use of a well-equipped opera house and substantial financial backing.

Another problem arises from the nature of the collaboration that produced them. Both ballets have a literary source, a scenario produced by a writer without the participation of a choreographer. Bartók worked only from an outline without the benefit of a detailed specification such as Tchaikovsky received from Petipa, or as Balanchine was to provide for Stravinsky. When writing *Duke Bluebeard's Castle*, the text constrained him to start straight into the action and to proceed with swift directness. This in no way reduced his ability to paint scenes and depict character — rather the opposite. Bartók had no such firm guide for the ballets, and was apparently unfamiliar with the speed of dance to convey its purpose. In consequence there is a disproportion of timing which compels a choreographer to pad out some sequences of the action with repetitions or irrelevancies. This is particularly true of *The Wooden Prince*, which has a running time close to that of *Bluebeard*. Although the *Mandarin* is more concise, there is still a risk of losing impetus during the attacks on the Mandarin, and of the melodrama becoming ludicrous.

The ballets in their time

The limited success of *The Miraculous Mandarin* and, even more, of *The Wooden Prince* on stage seems the more ignominious when compared with the place which *Duke Bluebeard's Castle* has found in the operatic repertory, or with the ballets which Stravinsky was writing during the same decade. Ravel's contemporaneous *Daphnis and Chloe*, however, indicates that musical quality is no guarantee of a ballet's success.

Comparison with Diaghilev's works sheds light on the reasons for the failure of Bartók's ballets. Indecency was the charge mainly levelled at *The Miraculous Mandarin*, yet Diaghilev was able with impunity to present *Thamar*, a subject with close parallels: the heroine offers one night of love to good-looking strangers who take her fancy, then has them killed. *Cleopatra*, too, had a strong sexual element, and one of his biggest successes, *Scheherezade*, showed an orgy in a harem followed by a massacre. These works gave his fashionable audiences a *frisson* and, although there were sometimes complaints on tour (in Spain, for instance, and America), these were welcomed by his publicists, and did not prevent him from presenting them over long periods. The difference is that *Mandarin* is set in a modern city, whereas Diaghilev's 'shocking' ballets were all distanced in time and place. When Nijinsky attempted some mildly improper innuendos in a contemporary setting with *Jeux*, they went unnoticed in the general confusion about his subject-matter, and it was not until the very different moral atmosphere of the 1920s that *Les Biches* offered its picture of lust at a smart contemporary house-party.

Even today, after decades in which choreographers have tried to relate ballet to modern life, it is rare to find a modern setting among the most successful works. Literature, history or biography are frequent sources of inspiration, resulting in a range of subjects from Spartacus through Romeo and Juliet to Manon. There have been exceptions, starting as far back as the oldest surviving ballets, Galeotti's *Whims of Cupid* and Dauberval's *La Fille mal gardée*, both from the 1780s, but also both comedies. Serious dance drama concerning people dressed like their audiences has always been harder to take. That is only partly a question of what people are used to. The strength and immediacy of emotions expressed in dance can be disturbing.

It was inevitable that *The Miraculous Mandarin* would experience problems in acceptance, with its subject of prostitution and murder in a contemporary setting, the woman presented (as music and scenario both make clear) without the glamour and discretion of her operatic sisters in *La traviata* or *La bohème*. But Lengyel's plot was a further problem. Its realism is undercut by the first two victims as conventional types, the comic old roué and the nervous young man. It is entirely disrupted by the Mandarin's arrival. Because the action does not work as straight drama, its value as allegory or metaphor is reduced.

It has been suggested that the subject Lengyel really wanted to tackle — but did not dare — was the death of Rasputin; inveigled to a rendezvous and then surviving attempts to kill him by poison and shooting, Rasputin was still alive when thrown into the river and eventually drowned. That grotesque fate is echoed in the attempts to suffocate, stab and hang the Mandarin. In any event, the force of the ballet lies in its suggestion of the power of strong desire; and its closing moments, of fulfilment and surrender, have been the saving grace of many otherwise unsatisfactory productions.

*

If *The Miraculous Mandarin* was condemned for indecency, the fault of *The Wooden Prince* is excessive innocence. Béla Balázs' scenario gives the choreographer little substance. Its naîvety may be perceived as a deliberate attempt to create a work that the management of the Budapest Opera could not object to, but the process surely went too far.

It is possible to find similarly negligible subject matter in the Diaghilev repertoire: *Le Pavillon d'Armide*, for instance, concerns a Gobelins tapestry which comes to life in a dream (with a hint at the end that it was not after all a dream). *Le Dieu bleu* is another example, devised by Cocteau to give Nijinsky an exotic role as Krishna intervening to save a girl who has been condemned to death. The novelty value of the company in its early years, the splendour of the designs and the presence of some exceptionally gifted dancers helped temporarily to mask the deficiencies of such works, but even so they did not survive.

The advantage of *The Wooden Prince* is the quality of Bartók's score over those of Nicolas Tcherepnin or Reynaldo Hahn. During the 1920s Diaghilev was to demonstrate with *Les Noces* (Stravinsky) and *Les Biches* (Poulenc) that, given good music and good choreography, minimal narrative content is no obstacle to a ballet's success. But *The Wooden Prince* has unfortunately never inspired choreography of the quality which Nijinska provided for Diaghilev. It is difficult to believe that it ever will, because the music is so graphically tied to the story, and the story is so silly. The problem is not just that this is a fairy-tale ballet conceived at a time when fairy-tales seem old-fashioned in the theatre. After all, Stravinsky's *Le Baiser de la fée* has survived. But *Baiser*, like the best of the nineteenth-century fairy-tale ballets, can be read as an allegory. Commentators have suggested 'poetic' meanings for *The Wooden Prince*, and tied themselves in knots doing so.

Consider a story based on the idea of a handsome young prince deciding that he needs to dress up a stick in his own cloak and crown in order to catch a pretty princess's attention. Compound that with his happening to have about his person a pair of scissors with which to cut off all his hair. Spin that out to an hour's length with dances for trees, waves, flowers, etc.. None of this is likely to excite the imagination of a creative choreographer; but even if it does, the anomalous nature of the fairy's role militates against any plausibility in the theatre, since her function in the drama is to bring the two lovers together but the process is one of keeping them apart. To suggest, as has been done, that this is a metaphor for the need for perseverance, or for loving the person not the finery, seems thin when the action is so arbitrarily contrived.

'The Wooden Prince' on stage

The choreographer is faced with a score that is large in duration and orchestration, but only four characters (never all on stage at once) supplemented by episodic entries for the *corps de ballet*. The set dances offer strong rhythmic support; the connecting links for the narrative have a more shimmering effect. Bartók's admiration for Richard Strauss is easy to deduce, but there are passages that can be compared to the Stravinsky of *The Firebird*, and naturally a strong reliance on Magyar dance and music traditions.

Harangozó's production was a straight-forward staging. It relied heavily on mime for the story-telling, and the solos seemed both fragmentary and conventional, while the symbolic intentions of the *corps de ballet* ensembles made for a muddled effect, except when the stream came to life (in this production it was shown as a moat protecting the Princess's castle). The most positive element of the choreography was the title role, which began with the dancer camouflaged against a tree, ready to be 'cut out', and included an amusingly eccentric duet with the Princess. By the time it was shown in Britain, the designs had been updated (by Zoltán Fülöp) from the presumably conventional original; by painting the scenery in the naive manner of a child's story book, and putting the dancers into accessorised tights instead of more naturalistic costumes, it added a charm the ballet would otherwise have lacked.

The only British production (London Festival Ballet) was also dominated by its design. Philip Prowse's costumes imposed an oriental flavour (for which there was no clear reason) and the hints of various eastern theatre traditions in Geoffrey Cauley's choreography did not impose a coherent style. The whole concept looked like decoration applied to distract the eye from the ballet's weakness.

László Seregi's current production for Budapest is the most successful attempt to present the ballet for modern audiences. The scenery by Attila Csikós puts a great structure on the stage, shaped with petals which can open and close; it provides a platform for some of the action. Otherwise the stage is bare — no castles — and the action is handled almost abstractly. In effect, he changes it from a narrative ballet to something closer to the 'symphonic ballets' popular in the 1930s, where an element of drama arising from the music is infused into the dance patterns. This allows the performers some virtuosity and as much humour as the piece will bear (the music expects this for the title role). Seregi has, to a large extent, made the ballet work by getting as far away as possible from anything its author and composer could have expected when they wrote it.

'The Miraculous Mandarin' on stage

In *Mandarin* the choreographer has a stronger, better organised basis to work from but one that invites — even demands — melodrama. The music is full of contrasts: from the sinisterly quiet and sinuous tune that illustrates the Girl's prowling, to climaxes of heavily accented rhythms and overwhelming volume; from the sarcastic tone with which Bartók depicts the old Beau, to the horrific announcement of the Mandarin's arrival and the frenzy of the final episodes. There is no possibility of treating this score abstractly; it is unavoidably programme music.

The Harangozó and Seregi productions differ more in emphasis than in kind. The former sets up a kind of sordid credibility (there was even a table lamp beside the whore's bed), which turned from realism to fantasy with the Mandarin's arrival: there was a chilling punctuation mark in the action at that point as a curtain was drawn over the big back window, blocking out a view of skyscrapers and creating a claustrophic effect. Seregi began with a symbolic act of violence: the thugs threw knives at a target which, when removed, revealed the Girl's head. Both introduced a high degree of lasciviousness into the movement, which Seregi heightened by a costume combining street shoes and a leather jacket, worn with a leotard resembling black underwear.

Among the productions seen in Britain, the extremes of approach were represented by those from Gothenburg and Győr. Ulf Gadd (New Swedish Ballet) stripped away lavish production in favour of a flexible construction of grilles which the dancers moved around. He introduced swift brief changes of choreographic character even within episodes: from direct vicious drama to athletic rough-and-tumble, and even a kind of poetry. He thus departed from strict adherence to the music but offered a variety of tone.

Iván Markó, on the other hand, imposed a variant on the plot in his production for the Győr Ballet. He set it in a garage where a gang arrived in a van (rather realistically) with their loot and a woman they had abducted. She was drugged, then subjected to multiple rape, in which, in her stupor, she sometimes cooperated enthusiastically. Instead of a Mandarin, the miraculous figure was a strange avenger, born from her own rage, who set about slaughtering the gang. Despite powerful performances, this did not entirely convince.

When keeping to the intended scenario, it is crucial to make the Girl's tenderness for her victim credible, so as to prepare for the climactic moment of release which ends the Mandarin's desire and his life. The plaintive quality of her music helps this, and a choreographer who took particular advantage of it was Flemming Flindt. This was a stylised production, in a stark grey setting by Preben Hornung, with the thugs and the Mandarin made inhuman by masks (the Mandarin's is ripped off at the end to symbolise his release). The costumes avoided naturalism, especially for the Girl, dressed in a body-

Jan Minarik and Beatrice Libonati in Pina Bausch's modern dance version of 'Bluebeard',
Wuppertal, 1982. (photo: Ulli Weiss)

stocking with colour making a bikini shape round breasts and hips. Her slow,
half-crouching solos, her equanimity when handled like a commodity by the
thugs who manipulate her into position as bait for their trap, were expressive
both of her seductiveness and her unwillingness. Later came a mounting
horror at the mysterious customer's explosive stamps and jumps; he sat
watching her with burning eyes before beginning his pursuit. Impassive, even
in pursuit or in his fights with the gang, fired with a terrifying determination,
this Mandarin gave focus to one of the most convincing interpretations of a
ballet which attracts choreographers like moths to the bright flame of its
music, but too often scorches them with its intractable story.

Other Bartók ballets

While the works which Bartók wrote as ballets have a precarious existence on
stage, many of his orchestral or instrumental works have inspired choreographers. The American modern-dance choreographer Doris Humphrey was
a little ahead of the general trend in 1948 with her *Corybantics* to the *Concerto
for Two Pianos*. Herbert Ross's *Caprichos* in 1950 used the *Contrasts* for violin,
clarinet and piano for a set of dance sketches based on Goya drawings (for
American Ballet Theatre, and then The Royal Ballet).

The Bartók work which has inspired the greatest number of choreographers
is the *Music for Strings, Percussion and Celeste*: the first was Aurel von Milloss in
1951. Among the many who followed him were two Britons: Kenneth
MacMillan in *Journey*, which he made for Nora Kaye (American Ballet
Theatre, 1953), and Peter Darrell in *The Prisoners* (also 1953), one of his finest

dance-dramas (Western Theatre Ballet, and later elsewhere, including the Scottish Ballet). Darrell also used the Third Piano Concerto for *The Wedding Present* (1962) and the Fifth String Quartet for *Home* (1965) (both for Western Theatre Ballet). MacMillan chose the Sonata for Two Pianos and Percussion for *Rituals* (The Royal Ballet, 1975).

The long list of other choreographers using Bartók scores includes Maurice Béjart's adaptation of Sartre's *Huis Clos* under the title *Sonate à trois*, to the Sonata for Two Pianos and Percussion, and Birgit Cullberg's *Medea*, set to an arrangement of *Mikrokosmos* and other piano pieces.

'Bluebeard' as a ballet

All of these ballets represent the choreographer's conception of what drama might be developed from the music, but there is one example where the choreographer has taken Bartók's own subject as a source of inspiration. This is the dance-drama created by Pina Bausch for her Wuppertal Dance Theatre from *Bluebeard*, and it is a striking example of one work of art provoking another that completely transmutes the original.

The full German title translates as *On listening to a tape recording of Béla Bartók's opera 'Duke Bluebeard's Castle'*, and the central character is a man, alone in an empty room. Leaves have piled up against the window, almost completely blocking the light, and have seeped in all over the floor. With his overcoat pulled shabbily around him, the man hunches over a tape-deck built into a trolley. Obsessively he uses the rewind button: with interruptions and repetitions, the work lasts twice as long as the opera. With the music's aid, he is trying to relive the love he once felt.

The empty room becomes a battle-ground for the war between him (and numerous reincarnations of his past self) and the many incarnations of the woman he loved. The violence between them is real: a woman's head is abruptly, forcefully and repeatedly pushed down; a body is banged against the wall, its feet pulled so that it crashes forward; a finger is pushed into a doll's eye; women are swung round in a sheet. At times the characters literally run up the wall (thanks to hidden foot- or handholds in Rolf Borzik's realistic-looking set).

Sexual aspirations are sometimes presented as an object of ridicule: the phrase in the opera about Bluebeard's armoury is accompanied by the sight of a row of men in briefs proudly flexing their muscles. The effectiveness of both tears and laughter as a sexual come-on or a sexual put-down is strongly exploited. There is little conventional dance in the production, but a gripping mixture of naturalism, evocative images, striking groups and hazardously slow or fast movement, often of what seems real danger. The eye and the imagination are both held throughout.

Two versions of 'Bluebeard': above: Mechtild Grossman in the Wuppertal dance version (photo: Ulli Weiss); below: Ingvar Wixell as Bluebeard in the 1974 Frankfurt production of the opera (photo: Mara Eggert).

Klaus Michel Gruber's 1974 Frankfurt staging of 'Duke Bluebeard's Castle' designed by Max von Vequel. (photo: Mara Eggert)

Selective Discography *by David Nice* Most electrifying of current recordings offering the complete *Miraculous Mandarin* is Claudio Abbado's with the London Symphony Orchestra and Ambrosian Singers on a disc which also includes Bartók's *Two Portraits* and another hellraiser, Prokofiev's *Scythian Suite*, with the Chicago Symphony Orchestra (Deutsche Grammophon 410 598-2, CD only). A cooler, even more analytical appraisal, Pierre Boulez's, has yet to be reissued on Sony Classics in the Boulez Edition, which will also include his complete *Wooden Prince* (already available separately on Sony CD 44700) and *Bluebeard's Castle* (mid-1991). Neeme Järvi has recorded both ballets complete with the Philharmonia (the orchestra had never played *The Miraculous Mandarin* before) for Chandos, also for 1991 release.

Among numerous versions of the *Mandarin* Suite, the most convenient will be Hiroshi Wakasugi's with the Tokyo Metropolitan Symphony Orchestra on Denon — clean, spectacular recording — since it is coupled with the Suite from *The Wooden Prince* (Denon 00-1330, CD only). Antal Dorati's serviceable Detroit Symphony Orchestra recording of the complete *Miraculous Mandarin*, with the *Music for Strings, Percussion and Celesta*, has the advantage of being available on all three formats (Decca CD 411 984-2DH, LP 411 984-1DH and cassette 411 984-4DH).

Duke Bluebeard's Castle

Conductor Orchestra	*Kertesz* LSO	*Sawallisch* Bavarian State Orchestra	*Ferencsik* Hungarian State Opera Orchestra	*A. Fischer* Hungarian State Orchestra
Bluebeard	W. Berry	D. Fischer-Dieskau	Y. Nesterenko	S. Ramey
Judith	C. Ludwig	J. Varady	E. Obraztsova	E. Marton
CD number	(Decca) 414 167-2DH	(DG) 423 236-2	(Hungaroton) HCD12254	(Sony) CD 44523
LP number	(Decca) 414 167-1LE	—	—	(Sony) 44523
Tape number	(Decca) 414 167-4LE	—	—	(Sony) 40-44523

Selective Bibliography

The best English introduction to Bartók's music is by Paul Griffiths, in The Master Musicians series (Dent, 1984, 1988). It deals especially sympathetically with *The Wooden Prince* and offers a sharp and accessible account of all three stage works in the general context of Bartók's output. The composer's marvellous *Letters* were published by Faber in 1971 (ed. János Demény). A fine collection of photographs is introduced in the English-language edition of *Béla Bartók, His Life in Pictures and Documents* by Ferenc Bónis, Corvina Kiado, 1981 (special edition for the Bartók centenary).

Other monographs include Halsey Stevens, *The Life and Music of Béla Bartók* (OUP, New York, 1953, 1964) and Tibor Tallián, *Béla Bartók, The Man and His Work* (Corvina, Budapest, 1988). An exceptionally interesting collection of essays by many distinguished Hungarian musicologists and documents is contained in *Bartók Studies*, compiled and edited by Todd Crow (Detroit Reprints in Music, 1976, 1977); it includes (in translation) a classic interpretation by Bence Szabolcsi of *The Miraculous Mandarin*, and a memorial essay on Bartók by Lukács. Both these texts, like the translations of the ballet scenarios in this volume, first appeared in the admirable *New Hungarian Quarterly*, which is of great interest to English-language audiences for the arts in Hungary.

For further information about the Sunday Circle, Mary Gluck has written *George Lukács and his Generation* (Harvard, 1985).

For readers interested in the Bluebeard myth, Bruno Bettelheim in *The Uses of Enchantment* (Peregrine, 1978) and Robert Darnton's opening essay in *The Great Cat Massacre and other Episodes in French Cultural History* (New York, 1984; Penguin, 1985) include interpretations in more general discussions of fairy tales.

An anthology of Fino-Ugrian folk poetry, *The Great Bear*, translated by Peter Sherwood and Keith Bosley, is forthcoming; it will contain more specimens of ballads of the type Bartók knew.

Contributors

Simon Broughton is a writer and broadcaster with a special interest in the music of Eastern Europe, and is one of the co-editors of the forthcoming *World Music: The Rough Guide*.

Paul Banks is the librarian of the Britten-Pears Library, Aldeburgh, and has written extensively on early-twentieth-century music.

Mike Ashman has produced operas for The Royal Opera, Covent Garden, as well as for Welsh National Opera, Scottish Opera, Norwegian Opera, Dublin Grand Opera and the Royal College of Music.

Julian Grant's opera, *The Skin Drum*, won the 1988 National Opera Association of America's Best Chamber Opera Award.

John Lloyd Davies has made several operatic translations, and produced for English National Opera, Scottish Opera and Kent Opera, several productions in Vienna at the Kammeroper, and revivals in Frankfurt and Bregenz.

John Percival is the dance critic of *The Times*, and editor of *Dance and Dancers*.

Professor Ferenc Bónis is an acknowledged expert on the life and works of Béla Bartók.